W9-BAV-558

MODERN AMERICAN
LYRICS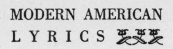

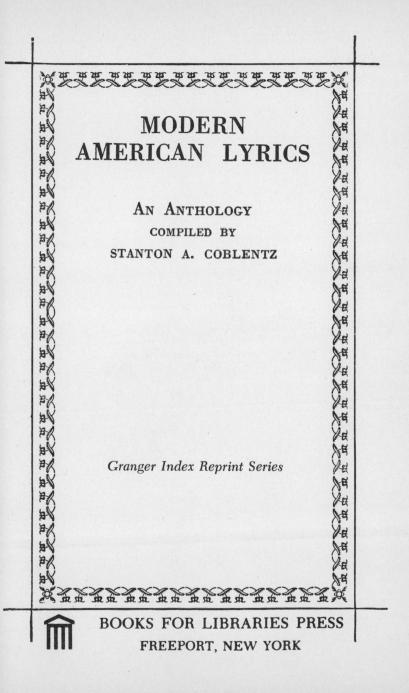

MODERN AMERICAN LYRICS

An Anthology

COMPILED BY

STANTON A. COBLENTZ

Granger Index Reprint Series

BOOKS FOR LIBRARIES PRESS
FREEPORT, NEW YORK

First Published 1924
Reprinted 1971

INTERNATIONAL STANDARD BOOK NUMBER:
0-8369-6281-8

LIBRARY OF CONGRESS CATALOG CARD NUMBER:
76-167476

PRINTED IN THE UNITED STATES OF AMERICA

PREFACE

In view of the present prevalence of anthologies, and in particular of anthologies of contemporary poetry, the compiler of a new collection of lyrics enters the field necessarily upon the defensive. "Why another anthology?" is the question with which he is certain to be assailed; and unless he can answer this challenge satisfactorily, unless he can show that his particular volume occupies some niche not filled by any other volume in existence, then explanation must inevitably give way to apologies, and he must crave pardon for having added a few more waste pages to the limbo of the unnecessary.

But it is not with an apology, nor even with a timid gesture of hesitation, that I venture to make public the accompanying selection of lyrics. Singularly enough, there seems to me to be not only a vacant place but a cavernous gap in the ranks of current poetic compilations; and, paradoxically, it is the very abundance of anthologies that makes an addition to the list not only desirable but necessary. Commendable as has been the work of recent anthologists, many compilers appear not to have been sufficiently discriminating in sorting the chaff from the wheat, the sand from the sugar, the thorns from the roses; they have allowed themselves to drift aimlessly with the uncertain poetic currents of the times, and have been so anxious to be liberal in their views and catholic in their preferences that they have momentarily lost sight of those fundamentals to which all true poetry must be anchored to-day no less certainly than in the times of Chaucer.

It is of course a truism that an anthology should contain good poetry; yet the reader whose ear has been attuned to graceful rhythms and whose mind has been made ready for exalted thoughts will find little satisfaction in much modern verse that is recommended as good. Page after page, he will discover, is devoted to formless effusions whose music is less than the music of dignified prose; page after page is filled with the sordid things of everyday, with kitchen sinks and bathtubs and cobblestones and loveless adulteries; and if in the interlude—as frequently occurs—one comes across a glowing sentiment or memorable melody or flash of imagination that reveals wide vistas of the sun-tinged storm-clouds or of the starry night-skies, then one is likely to be plunged on the next page into the monologue of a real estate agent if not into an epic of the hog-pens.

The whole question, of course, is fundamentally one of theory; but theory or no theory, I seriously object to turning from a finished lyric by George Sterling or Hermann Hagedorn to the raucous crudity of Alfred Kreymborg or of Carl Sandburg;

and I protest against finding a delicate love poem by Lizette Woodworth Reese sandwiched in between John V. A. Weaver's ungrammatical discourse on a Registered Pharmacist and one of Edgar Lee Masters' pseudo-Freudian disquisitions on sex. Both Mr. Masters' effort and Mr. Weaver's may be entirely appropriate in its place; but that place, in my opinion, is not in a book that purports to represent the best in contemporary poetry. While I can see no objection to a volume made up homogeneously of the work of the Imagists and Ultra-Modernists, yet I feel that it is inartistic as well as harmful and misleading to place the flippant irregularity of Marianne Moore or of William Carlos Williams side by side with the classic serenity of David Morton or the restraint and dignified charm of Thomas S. Jones. What is needed is not an anthology representative of all schools that claim to be writing poetry; what is needed is a volume based upon a clear-cut and definite conception of poetry and consistent in its attempt not to mix oil and water or to reconcile fire with ice. In my selection of lyrics I have been encouraged by the belief that such an anthology would not only fill an unoccupied place but would respond to a widely felt demand; I have been aided by the conviction that many superior poems have been overclouded if not altogether obscured by their unnatural association with the tawdry, the prosaic, and the ludicrous; and I have been actuated throughout by the view that, by the sheer excellence of its contents, a representative volume of verse in the older forms may constitute a forceful refutation of the poetic extremists.

This, of course, brings us to the question of what comprises good poetry; and, without attempting any protracted theoretical discussion, I may state that a good poem, in my conception, should first of all be musical in essence. For if there be anything fundamental to distinguish prose from poetry, it is the elevated, orderly, and sustained rhythm of the latter, a rhythm that serves the purpose not only of beauty but of effectiveness in imparting emotions and ideas, since in some not wholly explained fashion it seems to correspond with the rhythm of the subconscious. Secondly, in order to justify its designation as a special form of literature, poetry should deal only with subjects that cannot be treated equally well in prose; it should not be concerned with stone pavements and tenements, nor even with skylarks or the sunset, unless it can attain a distinctiveness of presentation impossible without the peculiar contrivances of verse. A high percentage of the best known modern poetry and so-called poetry, it appears to me, violates both these conditions; its tonal basis as often as not is the siren or the triphammer rather than the flute or the violin, and its subjects are those that any newspaper reporter might handle almost as well.

On the other hand, there is a considerable amount of excellent poetry that has virtually escaped attention. Part of it, doubtless, has been neglected because its creators happened to be poor and without influence or good luck; part of it, assuredly, has been overlooked because of the tendency of our intelligentsia to embrace radicalism in poetry because they favor radicalism in politics and to discard conventions in verse because they reject conventions in social life or in morality. It is largely this poetry, competent in workmanship and distinguished in subject-matter, that I have endeavored to represent in "Modern American Lyrics"; and it is my hope that I may succeed in calling attention to meritorious work that has not yet received its due meed of praise.

The reader will, of course, come across many names that are familiar and have in no wise been neglected by the critics or the public; he will discover that Edwin Arlington Robinson, Sara Teasdale, Witter Bynner, John G. Neihardt and others as widely known are represented by one or more poems each; but he will also be likely to make some new acquaintances among those who have not yet stood conspicuously in the light of publicity. In general, I have sought to confine myself to a moderate representation of the acknowledged leaders, whose work has been sufficiently heralded elsewhere; and where, as with Hermann Hagedorn and Arthur Davison Ficke, I have made as many as five or six quotations from authors frequently quoted before, I have been actuated by the conviction that the poet has received less recognition than his achievements merit.

With but one or two exceptions, the anthology is composed of the works of contemporary Americans who (so far as I know) are still alive. Alan Seeger and Joyce Kilmer, two notable poets that for all practical purposes are our contemporaries, have been omitted not only because they are no longer living but because their best poems have already been quoted almost to excess; Bliss Carman, C. G. D. Roberts and others have been disregarded because Canadian poets do not fall within the scope of my undertaking; and William Vaughn Moody, Richard Hovey and Madison Cawein have been excluded because they belong virtually to another generation. From among the poets represented, moreover, I have aimed to choose largely the pieces rarely if ever reprinted before; and while I have not made this an invariable rule, and have not refrained from selecting one or two well known although outstanding poems, such as Lizette Woodworth Reese's "Tears" and Edwin Arlington Robinson's "Richard Cory," yet, whenever possible without injustice to the author or loss to the reader, I have endeavored to represent poems not previously quoted.

Should the reader discover that his favorite author or poem is absent from the list, I must urge him to remember that the judgment of contemporary poetry is always largely a matter of opinion, and that I do not present my selections as infallible. By inadvertence or through ignorance I may have omitted the most deserving of living poets; all that I can plead is that I have represented only those who in my opinion are best worth representing, and that it is for the reader either to confirm or to reject my judgment. I do firmly believe, however, that the volume contains some excellent work by poets who have never been extensively anthologized: the vividness and beauty of the writings of Amory Hare, the imagination and pulsing strength of Edward H. Pfeiffer, the flawless lyricism of Brian Hooker, Kendall Banning, George Brandon Saul and others, all constitute a distinctive contribution that I am proud to be able to recommend.

It is a matter of some regret to me that certain poets have had to be omitted because of copyright difficulties. In order to meet any inquiries likely to arise, I may state that Edna St. Vincent Millay, acting through her agents, has refused to grant permission for the inclusion of any of her work; likewise that Robert Frost, in spite of his gracious willingness to be represented, has had to be excluded because of the prohibitive demands of his publishers. But to the great majority of publishers and authors, whose kindly aid and cooperation has made possible the publication of this anthology, I desire to express my thanks and to acknowledge my indebtedness.

S. A. C

New York, June, 1924.

CONTENTS

MODERN AMERICAN
LYRICS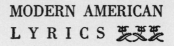

LIFE

Life is a shepherd lad who strides and sings
  Leading his flock, his brow bared to the sun,
Who knows the good grass and the hidden springs
  From whence streams of eternal beauty run.

Life is a cowherd, old, with bleeding lips,
  Driving fear-maddened cattle down a hill,
With matted hides worn raw at knees and hips,
  Knowing no sleep, no leisure to be still.

For one the dew, the hare-bell and the song;
For one the mire, the hurry and the thong.

Amory Hare.

1

TEARS

When I consider Life and its few years—
A wisp of fog betwixt us and the sun;
A call to battle, and the battle done
Ere the last echo dies within our ears;
A rose choked in the grass; an hour of fears;
The gusts that past a darkening shore do beat;
The burst of music down an unlistening street—
I wonder at the idleness of tears.
Ye old, old dead, and ye of yesternight,
Chieftains, and bards, and keepers of the sheep,
By every cup of sorrow that you had,
Loose me from tears, and make me see aright
How each hath back what once he stayed to weep;
Homer his sight, David his little lad!

Lizette Woodworth Reese.

CHARTINGS

There is no moon, only the sea and stars;
  There is no land, only the vessel's bow
  On which I stand alone and wonder how
Men ever dream of ports beyond the bars
  Of Finitude that fix the Here and Now.
A meteor falls, and foam beneath me breaks;
  Dim phosphor fires within it faintly die.
  So soft the sea is that it seems a sky
On which eternity to life awakes.

The universe is spread before my face,
  Worlds where perchance a million seas like this
  Are flowing and where tides of pain and bliss
Find, as on earth, so prevalent a place
  That nothing of their wont we there should miss.
The Universe, that man has dared to say
  Is but one Being—ah, courageous thought!
  Which is so vast that hope itself is fraught
With shame, while saying it, and shrinks away.

Shrinks, even as now! For clouds sweep up the
        skies
  And darken the wide waters circling round,
  From out whose deep arises the old sound
Of Terror unto which no tongue replies
  But Faith—that nothing ever shall confound.

3

Not only pagan Perseus but the Cross
    Is shrouded—with wild wind and wilder rain,
    That on me beat until my soul again
Sings unsurrendering to fears of Loss.

For this I know,—yea, though all else is hid
    Uncharted on the waters of our fate,
    All lands of Whence or Whither, whose estate
In vain imagination seeks to thrid,
    Yet cannot, for the fog within Death's gate,—
This thing I know, that life, whatever its source
    Or destiny, comes with an upward urge,
    And that we cannot thwart its mighty surge,
But with a joy in strife must keep the course.

Cale Young Rice.

LET ME LIVE OUT MY YEARS

Let me live out my years in heat of blood!
　Let me die drunken with the dreamer's wine!
Let me not see this soul-house built of mud
　Go toppling to the dust—a vacant shrine!

Let me go quickly like a candle light
　Snuffed out just at the heyday of its glow!
Give me high noon—and let it then be night!
　Thus would I go.

And grant me, when I face the grisly Thing,
　One haughty cry to pierce the gray Perhaps!
O let me be a tune-swept fiddlestring
　That feels the Master Melody—and snaps!

John G. Neihardt.

THE YEARS GO

On silver pinnacles I saw him stand
  And lift the starred black flagon of desire,
But that was in a far and ancient land,
  A morning-land of roses, song, and fire.
And O, the splendid gesture when he flung
  The emptied flagon down the whirling night
Grown mad and dizzy with the song he sung—
  The netted flame that bound his heart with light.

But now, in faltering silences, I see
  A broken thing whose thoughts are settled dust
And in whose eyes are time and agony,
  Who has no song to meet the future's thrust.
—He sits alone, his soul and passion thinned,
  There where on dwindled hills I see him weep,
And life's a dry horn withering down the wind
  That sweeps across the solitudes of sleep.

George Brandon Saul.

6

AS IN THE MIDST OF BATTLE

As in the midst of battle there is room
For thoughts of love, and in foul sin for mirth;
As gossips whisper of a trinket's worth
Spied by the death-bed's flickering candle-gloom;
As in the crevices of Caesar's tomb
The sweet herbs flourish on a little earth:
So in this great disaster of our birth
We can be happy, and forget our doom.
For morning, with a ray of tenderest joy
Gilding the iron heaven, hides the truth,
And evening gently woos us to employ
Our grief in idle catches. Such is youth;
Till from the summer's trace we wake, to find
Despair before us, vanity behind.

George Santayana.

THE BLACK PANTHER

There is a panther caged within my breast;
But what his name, there is no breast shall know
Save mine, nor what it is that drives him so,
Backward and forward, in relentless quest—
That silent rage, baffled but unsuppressed,
The soft pad of those stealthy feet that go
Over my body's prison to and fro,
Trying the walls forever without rest.

All day I feed him with my living heart;
But when the night puts forth her dreams and stars,
The inexorable Frenzy reawakes:
His wrath is hurled upon the trembling bars,
The eternal passion stretches me apart,
And I lie silent—but my body shakes.

John Hall Wheelock.

MEA CULPA

That man am I who wakes all night to mark
   The coming of the dawn, and lest it creep
   Past his closed eyes, he listens for the sheep
   To bleat, the cock to crow, the dog to bark;
And then, ere the upspringing of the lark
   His vigil weakens and he falls asleep,
   Nor does he waken till the sun is steep
   Into the noon, and in his soul the dark.
Yet though his hope is lost and gone his task,
   Still he must rise and forth into the drawn
   Mute day, without a purpose, nor dares ask
Whither his path leads or the reason why,
   Save that love stayed when all passed with the
      dawn.
   Lord, even as that foolish man am I.

                   Arturo Giovannitti.

THE VALLEY OF THE SHADOW

There were faces to remember in the Valley of
the Shadow,
There were faces unregarded, there were faces to
forget;
There were fires of grief and fear that are a few
forgotten ashes,
There were sparks of recognition that are not for-
gotten yet.
For at first, with an amazed and overwhelming
indignation
At a measureless malfeasance that obscurely willed
it thus,
They were lost and unacquainted—till they found
themselves in others,
Who had groped as they were groping where dim
ways were perilous.

There were lives that were as dark as are the fears
and intuitions
Of a child who knows himself and is alone with
what he knows;

10

There were pensioners of dreams and there were
    debtors of illusions,
All to fail before the triumph of a weed that only
    grows.
There were thirsting heirs of golden sieves that held
    not wine nor water,
And had no names in traffic nor more value than
    their toys:
There were blighted sons of wonder in the Valley of
    the Shadow,
Where they suffered and still wondered why their
    wonder made no noise.

There were slaves who dragged the shackles of a
    precedent unbroken,
Demonstrating the fulfillment of unalterable
    schemes,
Which had been, before the cradle, Time's inex-
    orable tenants
Of what were now the dusty ruins of their father's
    dreams.
There were these, and there were many who had
    stumbled up to manhood,
Where they saw too late the road they should have
    taken long ago:
There were thwarted clerks and fiddlers in the
    Valley of the Shadow,
The commemorative wreckage of what others did
    not know.

And there were daughters older than the mothers
    who had borne them,

11

Being older in their wisdom, which is older than
the earth;
And they were going forward only farther into
darkness,
Unrelieved as were the blasting obligations of their
birth;
And among them, giving always what was not for
their possession,
There were maidens, very quiet, with no quiet in
their eyes;
There were daughters of the silence in the Valley
of the Shadow,
Each an isolated item in the family sacrifice.

There were creepers among catacombs where dull
regrets were torches,
Giving light enough to show what was there upon
the shelves—
Where there was more for them to see than pleasure
would remember
Of something that had been alive and once had been
themselves.
There were some who stirred the ruins with a solid
imprecation,
While as many fled repentance for the promise of
despair:
There were drinkers of wrong waters in the Valley
of the Shadow,
And all the sparkling ways were dust that once had
led them there.

There were some who knew the steps of Age incredibly beside them,
And his fingers upon shoulders that had never felt the wheel;
And their last of empty trophies was a gilded cup of nothing,
Which a contemplating vagabond would not have come to steal.
Long and often had they figured for a larger valuation,
But the size of their addition was the balance of a doubt;
There were gentlemen of leisure in the Valley of the Shadow,
Not allured by retrospection, disenchanted, and played out.

And among the dark endurances of unavowed reprisals
There were silent eyes of envy that saw little but saw well;
And over beauty's aftermath of hazardous ambitions
There were tears for what had vanished as they vanished where they fell.
Not assured of what was theirs, and always hungry for the nameless,
There were some whose only passion was for Time who made them cold;
There were numerous fair women in the Valley of the Shadow,

13

Dreaming rather less of heaven than of hell when
  they were old.

Now and then, as if to scorn the common touch
  of common sorrow,
There were some who gave a few the distant pity
  of a smile;
And another cloaked a soul as with an ash of
  human embers,
Having covered thus a treasure that would last him
  for a while.
There were many by the presence of the many
  disaffected,
Whose exemption was included in the weight that
  others bore:
There were seekers after darkness in the Valley
  of the Shadow,
And they alone were there to find what they were
  looking for.

So they were, and so they are; and as they came
  are coming others,
And among them are the fearless and the meek
  and the unborn;
And a question that has held us heretofore without
  an answer
May abide without an answer until we all have
  ceased to mourn.
For the children of the dark are more to name than
  are the wretched,
Or the broken, or the wearied, or the baffled, or
  the shamed:

There are builders of new mansions in the Valley
of the Shadow,
And among them are the dying and the blinded and
the maimed.

Edwin Arlington Robinson.

GHOSTS

You have familiar faces and warm hands,
    You kindly women and you friendly men
That speak to me from long-remembered lands
    That I have known and shall not know again.

You do not know that you are ghosts of dreams
    That once were flesh and blood,—you do not
        know
That you have no more being than bright gleams
    Of winter sunlight on deep-drifted snow.

You cannot see what valleys and what hills,
    You cannot see what sounding oceans lie
Between us in this room that laughter fills,
    The while we greet and talk and say good-bye.

When you have buried what remains of me
    In the brown earth below the wind-swept grass,
Cold carven marble will your witness be
    That you were with me then, and saw me pass.

One year from now, perhaps, or twenty more,
    You will attend me on that last gray ride
And never know you did not close the door,
    And never know how long ago I died.

Harold Trowbridge Pulsifer.

AS IN A ROSE-JAR

As in a rose-jar filled with petals sweet
Blown long ago in some old garden place
Mayhap, where you and I, a little space
Drank deep of love and knew that love was fleet;
Or leaves once gathered from a lost retreat
By one who never will again retrace
Her silent footsteps—one whose gentle face
Was fairer than the roses at her feet;

So, deep within the vase of memory
I keep my dust of roses fresh and dear
As in the days before I knew the smart
Of time and death. Nor aught can take from me
The haunting fragrance that still lingers here—
As in a rose-jar, so within my heart.

Thomas S. Jones, Jr.

THE EYES OF GOD

I see them nightly in my sleep.
The eyes of God are very deep.
There is no cave, no sea that knows
So much of unplumbed depth as those,
Or guards with walls or spectres dumb
Such treasures for the venturesome.

I feel them burning on my back.
The eyes of God are very black.
There is no substance and no shade
So black as God His own eyes made;
In earth or heaven no night, no day
At once so black, so bright as they.

I see them wheresoe'er I turn.
The eyes of God are very stern.
The eyes of God are golden fires
That kindle beacons, kindle pyres;
And where like slow moon-rays they pass
They burn up dead things as dry grass.

They wait, and are not hard to find.
The eyes of God are very kind.
They have great pity for weak things
And joy in everything with wings;
And glow, beyond all telling bright,
Each time a brave soul dares a flight.

Hermann Hagedorn.

AUDIENCES

Within, the dazzling lights are hushed and low.
The music sinks to a faint breathlessness;
There is a rustling of a woman's dress,
A child cranes forward, listening; row on row
Of strained, exalted faces seem to glow
Like white flames in the dusk with sharp distress,
Beholding Juliet dead; the aching press
Of pain stabs the dry throat and will not go.

Without, swung in illimitable space,
Across the soundless stage the planet runs;
Gigantically like shadows on the waste
And silence of the night, the high gods lean,
Shoulder to shoulder, peering on the scene
Across the footlights of the spinning suns.

Howard Mumford Jones.

19

Three days I heard them grieve when I lay dead.
(It was so strange to me that they should weep!)
Tall candles burned about me in the dark,
And a white crucifix was on my breast,
And a great silence filled the lonesome room.

I heard one whisper, "Lo, the dawn is breaking,
And he has lost the wonder of the day."
Another came whom I had loved on earth,
And kissed my brow and brushed my dampened
          hair.
Softly she spoke, "O that he should not see
The April that his spirit bathed in! Birds
Are singing in the orchard, and the grass
That soon shall cover him is growing green.
The daisies whiten on the emerald hills,
And the immortal magic that he loved
Wakens again—and he has fallen asleep."
Another said: "Last night I saw the moon
Like a tremendous lantern shine in heaven,
And I could only think of him—and sob.
For I remembered evenings wonderful
When he was faint with life's sad loveliness,
And watched the silver ribbons wandering far

Along the shore, and out upon the sea.
Oh, I remembered how he loved the world,
The sighing ocean and the flaming stars,
The everlasting glamour God had given—
His tapestries that wrap the earth's wide room.
I minded me of mornings filled with rain
When he would sit and listen to the sound
As if it were lost music from the spheres.
He loved the crocus and the hawthorn-hedge,
He loved the shining gold of buttercups,
And the low droning of the drowsy bees
That boomed across the meadows. He was glad
At dawn and sundown; glad when Autumn came
With her worn livery and scarlet crown,
And glad when Winter rocked the earth to rest.
Strange that he sleeps to-day when Life is young,
And the wild banners of the Spring are blowing
With green inscriptions of the old delight."
I heard them whisper in the quiet room.
I longed to open then my sealèd eyes,
And tell them of the glory that was mine.
There was no darkness where my spirit flew,
There was no night beyond the teeming world.
Their April was like Winter where I roamed;
Their flowers were like stones where now I fared.
Earth's day! it was as if I had not known
What sunlight meant! . . . Yea, even as they
        grieved
For all that I had lost in their pale place,
I swung beyond the borders of the sky,
And floated through the clouds, myself the air,
Myself the ether, yet a matchless being

21

Whom God had snatched from penury and pain
To draw across the barricades of heaven.
I clomb beyond the sun, beyond the moon;
In flight on flight I touched the highest star;
I plunged to regions where the spring is born,
Myself (I asked not how) the April wind,
Myself the elements that are of God.
Up flowery stairways of eternity
I whirled in wonder and untrammeled joy,
An atom, yet a portion of His dream—
His dream that knows no end . . .
                              I was the rain,
I was the dawn, I was the purple east,
I was the moonlight on enchanted nights,
(Yet time was lost to me); I was a flower
For one to pluck who loved me; I was bliss,
And rapture, splendid moments of delight;
And I was prayer, and solitude, and hope;
And always, always, always I was Love.
I tore asunder flimsy doors of time,
And through the windows of my soul's new sight
I saw beyond the ultimate bounds of space.
I was all things that I had loved on earth—
The very moonbeam in that quiet room,
The very sunlight one had dreamed I lost,
The soul of the returning April grass,
The spirit of the evening and the dawn,
The perfume in unnumbered hawthorn blooms.
There was no shadow on my perfect peace,
No knowledge that was hidden from my heart.
I learned what music means; I read the years;
I found where rainbows hide, where tears begin;

I trod the precincts of things yet unborn.
Yea, while I found all wisdom (being dead),
They grieved for me. . . . I should have grieved
    for them!

Charles Hanson Towne.

LIFE

There was a low, dull droning in my ears,
  I saw faint bodies bended, dim and gray,
And faces soft behind a blur of tears.
  Cold lights like weary stars hung far away.

And muffled voices pelted me like rain.
  I hardly heard and did not understand.
White lips about me seemed to cry with pain.
  From every shadow poured a stretching hand.

There was a scent of roses lost in smoke.
  A famished taste grew ghostly in the air,
And shapes untouched like bubbles soared and
      broke . . .
  There was a haunting vagueness everywhere.

Then through the shapes a wave of motion went.
  Toward me they came and never turned aside.
Through me they passed . . . I knew not what it
      meant,
  And then I half remembered I had died.

Edward H. Pfeiffer.

24

I SOMETIMES WONDER

I sometimes wonder if the roses grow
    Faint-hearted in the blinding summer sun,
Waiting the slow, unerring hand of time,
    The grief of petals falling one by one.

I wonder if they envy dandelions
    Who spring to deepest being in a day,
And who, as little stars, come down from heaven,
    So riotously bloom and haste away.

I thought a frail rose murmured low to-day,—
    "Ah! when the first brief fragrancy is gone,
To be dispersed upon the flying breeze,
    Whirled with a song into oblivion!"

Amory Hare.

LONELINESS

The waning moon was up,—the stars
  Were faint, and very few;
The vines about the window-sill
  Were wet with falling dew;

A little cloud before the wind
  Was drifting down the west;
I heard the moaning of the sea
  In its unquiet rest;

Until, I know not from what grief
  Or thought of other years,
The hand I leaned upon was cold
  And wet with falling tears.

Ina Coolbrith.

THE MIST AND THE SEA

The mist crept in from the sea
  Out of the void and the vast;
And it bore the silver rain
A shimmering guest in its train,
And many a murmuring strain
  Of the ships that sailed in the past;
Soft as sleep's footfalls be
The mist crept in from the sea.

The mist crept in from the sea
  And folded the length of the shore
In the clasp of its mothering arms
As though it would shield from harms;
And lulled were the loud alarms,
  And lost was the rage and roar
Of the surge, so soothingly
The mist crept in from the sea.

The mist crept in from the sea,
  White, impalpable, strange;
Full of the wafture of wings,
Of eerie and eldritch things,
Of visions and vanishings
  Ever in shift and change;
Silently, hauntingly,
The mist crept in from the sea.

27

The mist crept in from the sea,
    And bode for a space, and then
It heard the imperious call
Of the deep, transcending all,
And it knew itself as the thrall
    Of the world-old master of men,
So, still as the dreams that flee,
The mist crept back to the sea.

Clinton Scollard.

ALDEBARAN AT DUSK

Thou art the star for which all evening waits—
O star of peace, come tenderly and soon,
Nor heed the drowsy and enchanted moon,
Who dreams in silver at the eastern gates
Ere yet she brim with light the blue estates
Abandoned by the eagles of the noon.
But shine thou swiftly on the sparkling dune
And woodlands where the twilight hesitates.

Above that wide and ruby lake to-West,
Wherein the sunset waits reluctantly,
Stir silently the purple wings of Night.
She stands afar, upholding to her breast,
As mighty murmurs reach her from the sea,
Thy lone and everlasting rose of light.

George Sterling.

ON HEARING A BIRD SING AT NIGHT

Out of what ancient summer of soft airs
    Was spun this song that stills each listening leaf—
This silver, moon-bright minstreling that fares
    Through all old time, still laden with a grief?
Some hidden bird, by turrets and black bars,
    Where one had languished for her face was fair,
Heard thus some troubadour beneath the stars,
    And learned this song of vanished hands and hair.

Who knows what golden story first gave birth
    To this old music that is heavy-sweet
With gardens long forgotten of the earth,
    With passion that was silver wings and feet,
To cross the silent centuries and be heard,
Calling again in this dream-troubled bird!

David Morton.

THE TREES THAT LEAN OVER WATER

The trees that lean over water,
  Living enchanted days,
I have known them on quiet farmlands,
  I have seen them on golden bays;
Dreaming in calm, cold twilights,
  Musing in noonday suns—
There are trees that lean over water
  Wherever the water runs.

There is nothing in days or seasons
  These rapt trees ever know;
The only world for their dwelling
  Is the crystal world below.
They are deaf to the wind's alluring,
  They are dumb through its stormy song;
They answer only the water
  That whispers and glides along.

The trees that lean over water,
  They miss the untroubled sky;
They lose its fathomless splendor
  As the starry march goes by;
In their own boughs entangled
  They view the eternal suns.

—There are trees that lean over water
  Wherever the water runs.

                    Marion Couthouy Smith.

31

HILL HUNGER

I think that something in the hill child dies
  When he is taken to the level lands.
The man bred by an ocean understands,
And he will tell you that his sick heart sighs
For hiss of surf—and all his being cries
  For roar of waves, and spray upon his hands:
  Ever beneath his weary feet the sands—
Ever a sail before his searching eyes.

And so I think the hill child always sees
  That broken line inked in against the skies,
Where saffron sunset drops to meet the trees
  Upon the hill tops—and the night hawk flies—
And when his mind cannot recapture these
  I think that something in the hill child dies.

Lillian Mayfiel`c` Roberts.

HAWAIIAN HURRICANE

Thunder and booming down within the womb
Of hollow earth, that grows and dims and dies;
Apart the stars are rushing; the night skies
Are flecked with white and drenched in foam and
    spume.
The lawn is strewn with briars. In the flume
I hear the crashing cane, and there are cries
Of wounded birds that fall to earth and rise
One-winged; and tall black palms thresh in the
    gloom.

Oh, Tempest, take me in Thy bold embrace!
More lover, Thou, than men whose voices fret
Against their ills. In storm, wind round me wet
White arms—my sad confuséd sense erase:
I know not mankind, nor know Thee, and yet
More love Thy majesty than any face.

Genevieve Taggard.

THE SKY IS GRAY AND SILENT

The sky is gray and silent and withdrawn
From the cold earth. A hundred frightened birds,
Like black, blown leaves, are battling down the
    wind.
The trees, like black, blown laces, too, are flung
Against the somber garment of the dusk.
The hills, protesting, drab and still to-night,
To-morrow shall be radiant in white.

I have come in from running with the wind—
The mad, cold wind that stings me with delight!
The wind that frees my blood and fires my brain
With the quick consciousness of new desire
For things unnamed of little human lips.

I am come in unto a futile fire,
And these close comforts that to-night, somehow,
I cannot brook! When I have closed the door
Against the wild encroachments of that wind,
I want to turn again and fling it wide,
And stretch my arms, and bid its fury sweep
Into the corners of these careful walls
And smite them with a prescience of the vast—
The boundless Unattained that waits for me.

34

But, no. I am come in. The door is shut.
I shall sit down before the ample fire
That good folk think should satisfy my need.
Have I not shelter, bread, and books to read?

But I am gray and silent and withdrawn
Like the cold sky. A chill unfallen snow
Chains my free spirit with its frozen breath.
See! through my window the unprisoned birds
Battle the blessèd wind that honors them!
And I sit fettered here—beside a fire.

Barbara Young.

THE SEA DREAM

To-night the loud waters, the loud and crying
    waters, the wild and silvered waters of the sea
    are in my mind,
Their booming and their thundering on sands the
    waves are plundering, the high foaming combers
    in charging ranks aligned.
I strip on the shingle and I race to the kiss of them,
    the cold beryl welter of wave on swelling wave,
The desperate rush and hiss of them, the drenching,
    blinding bliss of them, the kingly roaring
    waters, so strong my soul to save!

Oh, high along the sands, where nods not any
    flower, the silver, crumbling moon lights the
    silver webs they spread!
With passion, with power she sways their splendid
    hour, and a man's heart leaps to meet them, as
    quickened from the dead.
I slough the gray, ungracious and soiled and tat-
    tered seeming of the might that was my mind.
    Now, oh, better far to be
At dawn afloat and dreaming where the sea-birds
    waken screaming on the green gleaming rollers
    far out, far out at sea!

For there is deep silence from all the wrangling
   voices, and there is clean rapture undaunted by
   desire,
Where the world swings and poises, and the flashing
   blue rejoices, and, misty on the sea-line, some
   foreland glints with fire,—
With fire aripple around me, as the magic sun and
   blinding sweeps high through mists of rose, and
   the smell of dawn grows keen.
Time's mills, for their grinding, must wait upon my
   finding, ere I return to cities to sing what I
   have seen!

To sing of the faces that meet the midnight swim-
   mer who breasts the billows strongly through
   silver sequins bright
Till moonbeams filter dimmer, and white the faces
   glimmer of mermen and mermaids around him
   in the night,
With conch-shells spumy blowing and moonshine
   tresses flowing, and green eyes, and gray eyes,
   and lips like coral wet,
All gleaming and glowing, and seines phantasmal
   throwing to maze the breathing human in many
   a ghostly net;

To sing of that spirit who brings the breeze ere
   dawning; a cloud-enfolded angel, a flash of
   jeweled wings;
Who clears night's sable awning from waves that
   shudder fawning to heel, like hounds that
   scuffle about the feet of kings;

To sing of haunted waters, of sacred, moon-drenched
   waters, the gold of morning waters,—that fade
   away in light. . . .
For walls are still around me.   The dawn hath only
   found me a thrall to iron cities, sea-dreaming
   through the night!

William Rose Benét.

ISLAND BORN

I

My mother bore me in an island town,
So I love windy water and the sight
Of luggers sailing by in thick moonlight—
I wear the sea as others wear a crown.
My mother bore me near the spinning water,
Water was the first sound upon my ears,
And near the sea her mother bore her daughter,
And there were windows looking on the weirs.

Ever a wind is moaning where I go,
I never stand at night upon a quay,
But I must strain my eyes for sails that blow,
But I must strain my ears to hear the sea.
My mother bore me in an island town—
I wear the sea as others wear a crown.

II

My mother loved the way of ships that go
Out to the sea, their bows against the foam;
She loved the way of ocean mews and so
It was not strange an island was my home,
Or that I cried first in an island town,

Or in a sea town sought my earliest words.
My mother loved the sight of foggy boughs,
She loved the crying of out-going birds.

My mother's folk have many things to tell
Of vessels that went by the village inn,
The sudden clanging of the lighthouse bell,
The talk of seamen and the yarns they spin.
My mother loved reef water and the foam:
It was not strange an island was my home.

Harold Vinal.

ATAVISM

I leant out over a ledging cliff and looked down into
    the sea,
Where weed and kelp and dulse swayed, in green
    translucency;
Where the abalone clung to the rock and the star-
    fish lay about,
Purpling the sands that slid away under the silver
    trout.

And the sea-urchin too was there, and the sea-
    anemone.
It was a world of watery shapes and hues and
    wizardry.
And I felt old stirrings wake in me, under the tides
    of time,
Sea-hauntings I had brought with me out of the
    ancient slime.

And now, as I muse, I cannot rid my senses of the
    spell
That in a tidal trance all things around me drift
    and swell
Under the sea of the Universe, down into which
    strange eyes
Keep peering at me, as I peered, with wonder and
    surmise.

Cale Young Rice.

41

WONDER AND A THOUSAND SPRINGS

Along the just-returning green
That fledges field and berm and brake
The purple-veined white violets lean,
   Scarcely awake;

And pear and plum and apple trees,
Evoked to bloom before they leaf,
Lift cloudy branches filled with bees
   Strange as new grief.

A thousand springs will poise and pass
And leave no track beneath the sun:
Some gray-eyed lad, cool-cheeked as grass,
   Will watch each one,

And wonder, as I wonder here,
And find no clue I have not found,
And smile before he joins me, near
   But underground.

        William Alexander Percy.

BROKEN DREAMS

Why should I cling to my broken dreams,
    Tears, and the bitter, starless night,
The empty house on the lonely road,
    Whence love so long ago took flight?

Why should I cling to those fragrant hours,
    Like withered rose-leaves, faint and old,
When spring is singing again to me
    From laughing hills of green and gold?

I cannot tell what makes me turn
    From April's voice to dreams long dead;
But still I seek to nurse the wound,
    Whose pain but brings me tears instead.

                                    Morris Abel Beer.

NOCTURNE

Soft through a mist there's a memory creeping,
  To tell you in dreams that are wistful and low,
Soft through the mist between waking and sleeping—
  Of love as she came to you long, long ago. . . .

Tells you of love as a deathless maiden
  Who plays with a moonbeam and laughs like a
      child. . . .
Her eyes are how full!—and her lashes how laden
  With starlight!—her glances how level and mild!

See how her finger-tips fitfully glisten!
  See with what wonder her forehead is deep!—
She breathes, and you tremble . . . she waits, and
      you listen . . .
  She waits, and you breathe not . . . she breathes
      . . . and you sleep.

                                        Witter Bynner.

44

GHOST NIGHT

A hundred strange things
    Looked in at the door;
There went a soft foot
    Across the old floor.

Oh, lovely and lost,
    It was you who were there,
Wrapped round in the cloak
    Of your golden long hair!

The house grew as sweet
    As a just-lit flower,
On the edge of the rain,
    In an April hour.

Wrapped round in the cloak
    Of your golden long hair,
Oh, lovely and lost,
    It was you who were there!

I fell at your feet;
    Enough you were near,
Although but a ghost
    With the ghosts of the year!

Lizette Woodworth Reese.

THE LONELY GARDEN

I walked about your garden
  In the dew-drenched early day,
The sun hung o'er the mountains,
  The mist was like a spray.

The cardinals and robins
  Poured music on the air
But their songs were sorrow laden
  Because you were not there.

The grass upon the hillside,
  A mass of tangled gray,
Had lost its velvet greenness
  Because you were away.

The flowers in your borders
  Looked pale and wan to me;
They would not bloom their brightest
  Were you not there to see.

A flash of crimson beckoned
  From a corner quite apart;
Where choked by weeds and brambles
  I found a bleeding heart.

I bent my head in anguish
  To kiss the blood-red stain,
Libation for the Princess
  Who will not come again.

So I left my lonely garden
  While my wonder waked anew
That the sun should go on shining
  When the grass grew over you.

Virginia Taylor McCormick.

AT SUNSET

Love came across the meadows
  At the dawning of the day;
Before him fled the shadows,
  Past the mountains, far away;
Love came, a dear, unbidden guest;
The mated bird sang by its nest;
While morning caroled in my breast,
  And Oh, the joy of living!

Love came across the meadows
  At the dawning of the day,
But left me in the shadows
  When night fell, cold and gray;
He fled, the false and fickle guest;
The bird drooped by the empty nest;
The evening chilled my lonely breast,
  And Oh, the woe of living!

James B. Kenyon.

THIS DAY IS ALL A GREYNESS OF DIM RAIN

(From "Rue des Vents")

This day is all a grayness of dim rain.
Earth and the sky alike are wrapped in fold
Of the dim memory of some ancient pain,
Some wrong of bitter gods endured of old;
All gray and spent, save where I see you move
With lifted golden head and laughing eyes
And breast so delicate that no power but love
Could dwell there with his singing sorceries.
Proud little head, lifted amid the gloom!
Gay serious little heart, swift-running feet!
Into the shadowed broodings of this room
You bring the light of regions far and sweet.
Your laughter is a song, a golden beam
Out of the western rain-mist of my dream.

Arthur Davison Ficke.

NIGHT OF RAIN

Better the empty sorrow in the dark,
The crying heart, the crying eyes that stare
Blindly till morning, than the bitter glare
Of rainy street-lights, threaded spark to spark
To lure me from this room in my distress,
Out where you pass—far out beyond my sight.
Better to grope in this small space of night
For sleep, for peace, or any nothingness.

You are not here, and you will not return;
And if you came—the door is shut, and locked
And sealed with pride, and barred across with pain;
And now it is for quiet that I yearn. . . .
I should but lie and listen, if you knocked—
Rain in my heart, and at my window rain.

Bernice Lesbia Kenyon.

LOVE CAME BACK AT FALL O' DEW

Love came back at fall o' dew,
  Playing his old part;
But I had a word or two
  That would break his heart.

"He who comes at candlelight,
  That should come before,
Must betake him to the night
  From a barrèd door."

This the word that made us part
  In the fall o' dew;
This the word that brake his heart—
  Yet it brake mine, too.

Lizette Woodworth Reese.

SONNETS

(From "Out of Mist")

I

How shall I learn to live with this strange love
That has no place among the things I know?
For it is like a dream wherein I move
Upon a sea in whose strong undertow
I must succumb, save for some power of will
To battle with uncharted streams of death.
Ofttimes I struggle to recall that still
And brooding day when, with confiding breath,
I reached across the drifting sands to you
Whose strength was rock. But ah! how suddenly
That whirling cloud from out the unbroken blue
Swept us, unmindful, to the open sea,
Where, on relentless tides, moon-piloted,
We drift to shores of the forgotten dead.

II

How readily the dreaming mind forgives
The scar that glows relentlessly by day
And, in forgetfulness of pain, relives
The undimmed beauty of a far-off May.

52

Thus tenderly you came to me last night
And for one sleeping heart-beat held me near. . . .
One heart-beat whose far echo of delight
It seemed must ring from sphere to answering
    sphere.
Then suddenly I woke and you were gone
And once again the scar burned livid red.
How profitless my dream when with the dawn
I waken with a heart uncomforted
And, searching, know not if I grieve for hate
Or for a love that Hell cannot abate.

III

Here in the sanctuary of my dreams,
How many a bud shall flower when I am dead!
Ah, my belovèd, even now it seems
As if they bent and swayed above my head.
What though the skeptics proved that death were
    real
And you were gone from me a million years
Yet would some restless daffodil reveal
The image God re-captured from my tears.
And you, with silent lips forever cold,
Might vainly seek my hand across the dark
But some old dream would flash; that day would
    hold
At dusk the promise of the rainbow's arc. . . .
There is not any grave where love may rest
Until illusion crumbles in earth's breast.

Florence Kilpatrick Mixter.

THE MYSTERY

They who have loved too well—and been betrayed,
Tried in the fire and utterly dismayed,
   Strange, is it not, how they return to Love,
And bare their hearts to his great gleaming blade!

Charles Hanson Towne.

RED POPPIES IN THE WHEAT

Life is red poppies in the wheat,
  Love be not late!
Keen is time's sickle; years are fleet;
Life is red poppies in the wheat,
Filled with brave dreams and crimson sweet
  But bound by fate!
Life is red poppies in the wheat,
  Love be not late!

John Richard Moreland.

ONCE ON A TIME

Once on a time, once on a time,
  Before the Dawn began,
There was a nymph of Dian's train
  Who was beloved of Pan;
Once on a time a peasant lad
  Who loved a lass at home;
Once on a time a Saxon king
  Who loved a queen of Rome.

The world has but one song to sing,
  And it is ever new;
The first and last of all the songs,
  For it is ever true;
A little song, a tender song,
  The only song it hath:
"There was a youth of Ascalon
  Who loved a girl of Gath."

A thousand thousand years have gone,
  And eons still shall pass,
Yet shall the world forever sing
  Of him who loved a lass—
An olden song, a golden song,
  And sing it unafraid;
"There was a youth, once on a time,
  Who dearly loved a maid."

                    Kendall Banning.

YOUNG LOVE IS LIKE A ROSEBUD

Young love is like a rosebud
    That blushes to confess,
And fragrant is the rosebud,
    Each breath a soft caress;

Yet lonely, too, the rosebud
    And sad, for oft appears
Within its glistening dew-drops
    The wistful glow of tears.

Louis Fagon.

SONG

The skies are dimly bright, Love,
  The stars like pulses beat
That falter with delight, Love,
  And the breeze is maddening-sweet—
  The breeze is maddening-sweet!
Borne soft along its way,
  The sighs of sleepy flowers
  From bowers to dusky bowers
Its laden wings delay.

The world is hushed in shade, Love,
  And shadowed all my heart;
This night for us was made, Love. . .
  And we so far apart—
  And we so far apart!
Unheeded on my ear
  The folded whispers fall—
  In vain the shadows call,
Because thou art not here.

Brian Hooker.

THE FOUNTAIN

In a green garden of delight
A hidden fountain played all night,
A gray and moving ghost of sound
That floated over phantom ground,
Now near, now far, as the wind blew.
The fountain was my love for you;
The wind, your moods as light as air;
The black night was my love's despair.

Harry Kemp.

IN ARCADY BY MOONLIGHT

In Arcady by moonlight (where only lovers go),
There is a pool where fairest of all the roses grow.
Why are the moonlit roses so sweet beyond compare?
Among their purple shadows my love is waiting
    there.

To Arcady by moonlight the roads are open wide,
But only joy can enter, and only joy abide;
There is the peace unending that perfect faith can
    know,
In Arcady by moonlight (where only lovers go).

Kendall Banning.

MY LOVE WAS BORN WHEN STARS WERE DANCING

My Love was born when stars were dancing,
  The tide was high and the moon was full,
The surf was white and the sea-gulls glancing;
  So bright was she, and beautiful.

My Love was named when trees were tossing,
  When brooks ran, singing, toward the sea,
And brown trout leapt by the stony crossing;
  So slim and swift and glad was she.

My Love was wed when the spring was young,
  When the western sky was a painted splendor,
And the crescent moon by a thread was hung;
  So sweet was she, so wise and tender.

My Love was buried when snow was deep,
  And the moon sailed over the ghostly hill,
And I feared to stir, and I dared not weep;
  So mute was she, so white and still.

Amory Hare.

BEYOND A MOUNTAIN

Somewhere beyond a mountain lies
A lake the color of your eyes—
And I am mirrored like a flight
Of swallows in that evening-light.

Lovers eternal, side by side,
Closed in the elemental tide,
Nurture the root of every land—
So is my hand within your hand.

Somewhere beyond an island ships
Bear on their sails, as on your lips
You bear and tend it from the sun,
The blossom of oblivion.

Eternal lovers, in whom death
And reaching rains have mingled breath,
Are drawn by the same draught apart—
So is my heart upon your heart.

Somewhere beyond a desert rolls
An ocean that is both our souls—
Where we shall come, whatever be,
I unto you, you unto me.

Witter Bynner.

WHEN THE WIND IS LOW

When the wind is low, and the sea is soft,
    And the far heat-lightning plays
On a rim of the west where dark clouds nest
    On a darker bank of haze;
When I lean o'er the rail with you that I love
    And gaze to my heart's content;
I know that the heavens are there above—
    But you are my firmament.

When the phosphor-stars are thrown from the bow
    And the watch climbs up the shroud;
When the dim mast dips as the vessel slips
    Through the foam as it seethes aloud;
I know that the years of our life are few,
    And fain as a bird to flee,
That time is as brief as a drop of dew—
    But you are Eternity.

Cale Young Rice.

THE SEA-LANDS

Would I were on the sea-lands,
 Where winds know how to sting;
And in the rocks at midnight
 The lost long murmurs sing.

Would I were with my first love
 To hear the rush and roar
Of spume below the doorstep
 And winds upon the door.

My first love was a fair girl
 With ways forever new;
And hair a sunlight yellow,
 And eyes a morning blue.

The roses, have they tarried
 Or are they dun and frayed?
If we had stayed together,
 Would love, indeed, have stayed?

Ah, years are filled with learning,
 And days are leaves of change!
And I have met so many
 I knew . . . and found them strange.

But on the sea-lands tumbled
 By winds that sting and blind,
The nights we watched so silent
 Come back, come back to mind.

I mind about my first love,
  And hear the rush and roar
Of spume below the doorstep
  And winds upon the door.

                    Orrick Johns.

(From "Sonnets of a Portrait-Painter")

I

VIEW FROM HEIGHTS

I am in love with high far-seeing places
That look on plains half-sunlight and half-storm,—
In love with hours when from the circling faces
Veils pass, and laughing fellowship glows warm.
You who look on me with grave eyes where rapture
And April love of living burn confessed—
The gods are good!   The world lies free to capture!
Life has no walls!   O take me to your breast!
Take me,—be with me for a moment's span!—
I am in love with all unveilèd faces,
I seek the wonder at the heart of man;
I would go up to the far-seeing places.
While youth is ours, turn to me for a space
The marvel of your rapture-lighted face!

II

To-day, grown rich with what I late have won,
Across the dusk I reach my hand to you.
Cold as a leaf long pillowing a stone
Your hand takes mine, like something strange and
    new.
So soon grown careless? . . . No, for in your eyes
A tenderness still lives, half-shy, half-bold. . . .
Then sudden wisdom to my trouble cries:
I know you still my love, but not the old.
That which I loved and won now all is gone;
She was an hour, a moment, a swift mood,—
Vanished forever into deeps unknown,—
And a new creature rules your brain and blood.
Yesterday you were mine, beloved and fair.
To-day I seek,—another love is there.

III

What if some lover in a far-off Spring,
Down the long passage of a hundred years,
Should breathe his longing through the words I
    sing—
And close the book, dazed by a woman's tears?
Does it mean aught to you that such might be?
Ah! we far-seekers! . . . Surely thus were proved
From dream to deed the souls of you and me:—
Thus only were it real that we had loved.
Gray ghosts blown down the desolate moors of time!
Poor wanderers, lost to any hope of rest!
Joined by the measure of a faltering rhyme!
Sundered by deep division of the breast!
Sundered by all wherein we both have part;
Joined by the far-world seeking of each heart.

IV

THE TIDINGS

They brought me tidings; and I did not hear
More than a fragment of the words they said.
Their further speech died dull upon my ear;
For my rapt spirit otherwhere had fled—
Fled unto you in other times and places.
Old memories winged about me in glad flight.
I saw your lips of longing and delight,—
Your grave glad eyes beyond their chattering faces.
I saw a world where you have been to me
More than the sun, more than the wakening wind.
I saw a brightness that they could not see.
And yet I seemed as smitten deaf and blind.
I heard but fragments of the words they said.
Life wanes. The sunlight darkens. You are dead.

Arthur Davison Ficke.

SEA-CHANGE

You are no more, but sunken in a sea
Sheer into dream, ten thousand leagues, you fell;
And now you lie green-golden, while a bell
Swings with the tide, my heart; and all is well
Till I look down, and wavering, the spell—
Your loveliness—returns. There in the sea,
Where you lie amber-pale and coral-cool,
You are most loved, most lost, most beautiful.

Genevieve Taggard.

THE RETURN

When the last hearth fire drowses to the drone
Of an embered blow, I shall be standing there
In the warm shadow close behind your chair
Where the grave depth of quiet takes a tone
Of deeper, graver quiet from your own:
And should you feel a tenderness on your hair,
And on your eyes the hovering breath of prayer,
Be not afraid and make no startled moan.

For it is only I that am returned
To look on you and love you out of pain,
And it is but my hand on you again,
My blessing even through the darkness burned;
And should you feel the nearness of a tear
Over your lips, know that my lips are near.

Joseph Auslander.

71

WE NEEDS MUST BE DIVIDED IN THE TOMB

We needs must be divided in the tomb,
For I would die among the hills of Spain,
And o'er the treeless melancholy plain
Await the coming of the final gloom.
But thou—O pitiful!—wilt find scant room
Among thy kindred by the northern main,
And fade into the drifting mist again,
The hemlocks' shadow or the pines' perfume.
Let gallants lie beside their ladies' dust,
In one cold grave, with mortal love inurned;
Let the sea part our ashes, if it must.
The souls fled thence which love immortal burned,
For they were wedded without bond of lust,
And nothing of our heart to earth returned.

George Santayana.

TO ONE I LOVE

To one I love
  I have been all things beautiful.
I am the stars, the light, the breath,
The music of the world set forth for him;
And I am witchery, and even woe,
Woe of a quality akin to joy!
The thought of me is subtly intertwined
With twilight and the wheeling swallows' cry,
With doorways dimly lit; and darkening fields;
The long road's ending, and the lantern's gleam;
With huddled roofs adream beneath the moon.
For I am that by which he is reborn.
The dearness of the hearth by candle-light;
The mystery wherein two spirits blend;
I have the strange remoteness of the heavens
And yet the patient nearness of the grass.

Amory Hare.

OFFERINGS

If I could sing as no man ever sang—
  Find the red heart of that unspoken lore
  That all sweet sound is only hunger for,—
If I might call the moonlight on the sea,
  The river-lily's dream, the soul of dew,
To lead the voices of my harmony,
  I should have songs, O Love, to sing to you.

If I could love as no man ever loved—
  The seeking of the girl unsatisfied,
  The passion of the bridegroom for the bride,
The mother's wonder in her newborn son,
  The boy's fresh rapture in his life come true—
If I might compass all these loves in one,
  I should have love, O Love, to bring to you.

Brian Hooker.

ALTHOUGH I DECKED A CHAMBER FOR
MY BRIDE

Although I decked a chamber for my bride,
And found a moonlit garden for the tryst
Wherein all flowers looked happy as we kissed,
Hath the deep heart of me been satisfied?
The chasm 'twixt our spirits yawns as wide
Though our lips meet, and clasp thee as I list,
The something perfect that I love is missed,
And my warm worship freezes into pride.
But why—O waywardness of nature!—why
Seek farther in the world? I had my choice,
And we said we were happy, you and I.
Why in the forest should I hear a cry,
Or in the sea an unavailing voice,
Or feel a pang to look upon the sky?

George Santayana.

ANNIVERSARY

I wonder had you wept or had you smiled,
Could you have read the book of things to be
That summer dusk we sat beside the sea,
And, like the children that we were, beguiled
Our wiser sense to think that we but whiled
An hour away in casual company?
Could you have known what now is memory,
I wonder had you wept or had you smiled?

Men call you happy.   Boldly I believe
That year by year I see the gladness grow;
Yet care and pain and vigils bravely kept
Gauntly confront the joys.   That August eve
Could you have dreamed the pain the happiest know
I wonder had you smiled or had you wept?

Hermann Hagedorn.

NOT TILL THE TEMPLES OF OUR SECRET TRUST

(From "Epitaph for the Poet V")

Not till the temples of our secret trust
Are blown in mist across a rainy sky,
And music crumbles wholly into dust,
And carven marbles into silence die—
Not until what we dream and what we know
Are merged and made inseparably the same,
And beauty dead a hundred years ago
Ceases to haunt us with a living flame—
Not till the harvest of slow-ripening Time
Is brought in golden sheaves triumphant home
And planets round into the perfect rhyme
Of death after their million years aroam—
Not until then shall any strangeness move
From its fixed place the strangeness of our love.

Arthur Davison Ficke.

AS IN A PICTURE-BOOK

My mother died when I was young,
  Yet not too young to know
What terror round the dark halls clung
  That aching day of snow.

I knew she could not comfort me.
  I sat there all alone.
Cold sorrow held me quietly
  Dumb as a winter stone.

And yet I seemed to watch it all
  As in a picture-book:
The silent people in the hall,
  My father's frozen look,—

The heaped white roses, and my dress
  So very black and new.
I watched it without weariness. . . .
  Ah, how the snow-blast blew! . . .

.   .   .   .

To-night you say you love me:—me,—
  Who leap to love you. Lo,
I am all yours so utterly
  You need not speak, nor show

78

One sign, but I shall understand
　　Out to our life's last rim:
Out into death's uncertain land,
　　Gracious be it or grim.

I am all yours . . . And yet to-night
　　The old trick haunts me. Look!
I see your face, O new delight,
　　As in a picture-book.

Your face, your shape, the fire-lit room,
　　The red rose on the shelf,—
And, leaning to its passionate bloom,
　　Troubled with love, myself . . .

Oh, hold your hand across my eyes.
　　They have no right to see!
But now, as then, they are too wise.
　　They stare. They frighten me.

Fannie Stearns Davis.

WE LAUGHED AND PARTED, NEVERMORE
TO MEET

We laughed and parted, nevermore to meet
   In this fair world of April green and blue.
   The whimsical companionship was through,
The gay, light-hearted irterlude complete.
Rising from the green bank that was our seat,
   Jesting at life, as we were wont to do,
We laughed and parted, nevermore to meet
   In this fair world of April green and blue.
Why did I never say how passing sweet
   Had been the days that I had spent with you?
   I almost thought you felt the impulse too—
The chance was gone, and, rising to our feet,
We laughed and parted, nevermore to meet.

Alfred R. Bellinger.

INTENTIONS

So many things I meant to say
To please, to praise, to make you glad;
Such splendid chances have I had
And yet I let them slip away;
And now in shame I bow my head
For moments lost and words unsaid.

So many deeds I planned to do
To ease the road of your behest,
But while I loitered taking rest
Another hand has aided you;
And now my heart is pricked with pain
For castles reared and wrecked in vain.

So many songs I meant to sing
To spur you on to greater heights,
To cheer you on those lonely nights
When faith is weak and hope takes wing;
But while I tarried with my song
Your struggling soul grew true and strong.

Without my words you reached your goal,
Without my help you won your fight;
Without my song you chose the right
And love and beauty clothe your soul.
To-day my path is rough and long. . . .
I need your words, your deeds, your song!

John Richard Moreland.

81

I KNOW A QUIET VALE

I know a quiet vale where faint winds blow
The silver poplar-branches all awry,
And ne'er another sound comes drifting by
Save where the stream's cool waters softly flow,
Only wild-roses riot there and throw
Their perfume recklessly, the while on high
Great snowy clouds pillow the smiling sky
And cast frail shadows on the grass below.

All is the same, the summer stillness dreams
In idleness across the sunny leas,
Until for very drowsiness it seems
The wind has gone to sleep within the trees—
Yet we once laughed at what the years might bring,
And now I am alone, remembering.

Thomas S. Jones, Jr.

TIME LINGERS

Ah, many a dream has passed me,
  Or friend has torn my heart;
Time lingers, growing weary,
  But friends and dreams depart.

For dreams too long forgotten—
  For friends forsaken, dead,
There bends a feathery willow
  On many a quiet bed.

Dorothy Dow.

THREE POPLARS

Three poplars paused beside a brook
  Before the autumnal mountain,
Then bowed to me, and undertook
The dance of death and shone and shook
  Like waters in a fountain.

O, high the happy bosom heaves
  When love is in the dancer!
But life falls quiet as the leaves,
And soon the dance of death bereaves
  A lover of his answer.

Lightly a girl had danced away
  Her breath and all her laughter;
A boy went joining her one day;
And a little fellow, at his play,
  Saw them and followed after. . . .

And now three poplars poised and shook
  Like waters in a fountain
And, iridescent, undertook
The dance of death beside a brook
  Between me and the mountain.

Witter Bynner.

SEA LULLABY

The old moon is tarnished
  With smoke of the flood,
The dead leaves are varnished
  With color like blood,

A treacherous smiler
  With teeth white as milk,
A savage beguiler
  In sheathings of silk,

The sea creeps to pillage,
  She leaps on her prey;
A child of the village
  Was murdered to-day.

She came up to meet him
  In a smooth golden cloak,
She choked him and beat him
  To death, for a joke.

Her bright locks were tangled,
  She shouted for joy,
With one hand she strangled
  A strong little boy.

Now in silence she lingers
  Beside him all night
To wash her long fingers
  In silvery light.

Elinor Wylie.

85

WILLIE PITCHER

He is forgotten now,
And humble dust these thirty years and more,
He whose young eyes and beautiful wide brow
    My thoughts alone restore.

Dead, and his kindred dead!
And none remembers in that quiet place
The slender form, the brown and faunlike head,
    The gently wistful face.

And yet across the years
I see us roam among the apple-trees,
Telling our tale of boyish hopes and fears
    Amid the hurried bees.

When I am all alone
By the eternal beauty of the sea,
Or where the mountain's eastward shade is thrown,
    His face comes back to me—

A memory unsought—
A ghost entreating, and I know not why,—
A presence that the restless winds of thought
    Acknowledge with a sigh;

Till I am half content
Not any more the loneliness to know
Of him who died so young and innocent,
    And ah! so long ago!

George Sterling.

TO A CHILD—TWENTY YEARS HENCE

You shall remember dimly,
  Through mists of far-away,
Her whom, our lips set grimly,
  We carried forth to-day.

But when, in days hereafter,
  Unfolding time shall bring
Knowledge and love and laughter
  And trust and triumphing,—

Then from some face the fairest,
  From some most joyous breast,
Garner what there is rarest
  And happiest and best,—

The youth, the light, the rapture
  Of eager April grace,—
And in that sweetness, capture
  Your mother's far-off face.

And all the mists shall perish
  That have between you moved.
You shall see her you cherish;
  And love, as we have loved.

Arthur Davison Ficke.

IN MEMORIAM

I

I could not write to you when you were dying,
Even to cheer you, of the trivial things
That summer to an idle schoolboy brings;
I could not speak so when I knew you lying
Within death's shadow, bravely death defying;
Nor had I skill to touch more solemn strings.
So I was speechless with the grief that wrings
A spirit impotent, the end descrying.
Boyish I wrote at last, impulsively,
And spoke my sorrow from a loaded heart,
Hoping to lighten you of some small part
Of the dark burden of your misery.
And then you tore my very soul apart
For you, the dying, wrote to comfort me.

II

I could not speak then for I had no skill,
Nor knew the courageous spirit I had lost;
Now I guess darkly what the struggle cost,
When with your splendid strength and dauntless will
You met death face to face and fought until
The body broke. So in autumnal frost
I have seen oaks, their naked branches tossed
Against the heavens on a windy hill.

I cannot think the everlasting rest
And quiet of heaven is a just reward
For your keen spirit tempered like a sword;
Still would you seek to win a distant goal,
Still journey onward in a noble quest.
Strife is the guerdon for so strong a soul.

III

Often the iron of the winding stair
Clattered, as hastily with lusty shout
I mounted to your door, and passed without,
Till to your welcoming cry I entered there,
To ask for comfort in a schoolboy care,
To seek solution of a weighty doubt,
Or joyously to say the buds were out
And spring was coming with the quickened air.
Youth pays no heed to death, nor understands
That the day's happiness will ever change,
Or love and friendship fail; and I, a boy,
Held those dear moments in unfeeling hands,
Scattered and squandered them in thoughtless joy.
How precious are they now, how sad, how strange.

Theodore H. Banks, Jr.

ELEGY

Here shall rest unmoved through the waning seasons
One who knew and dreamed, and forgot in dream-
    ing;
Now alone the trees, who remembered always,
Are his companions.

They to whom he came for their silent healing,
They who ever gave of their ancient patience;
Now alone with them and the night-wind's crooning
Leave him forgotten.

Thomas S. Jones, Jr.

NUSTSCHA

I

Nustscha! If they have left one rock of you
Beside the spring, or where the gray hills rose
Whereon of old I climbed at daytime's close
To watch the twilight birds rise and pursue,
Then there is still one heart I may turn to.
My feet shall follow where my spirit goes,
And scan the footprints of the ancient crows
Who when I left the valley vanished too.
Oh rather would I bruise my naked feet
Pacing your leaden hills, and drink my drink
Out of the marsh beside the shattered dam
Than linger here where one may come to beat
Loud on my door and clamor, and I shrink
To open lest he see how poor I am.

II

We were so tender, and we were so young,
The gayety that boldened in my feet
Was in your rock and grass, and firm and fleet
They bore the morning, an heroic throng.
Over the gardens and the trees I flung
My voice, but you were just as quick to greet
The lightning in the cloud and the great beat
Of thunder on the hilltops lifting strong.

Did not your valley rise and fall with pride
When from an oaken bough one golden dawn
I sang like any bird on any tree
My song of songs? Oh, day went side by side
Over the forest with the new-born sun.
God give me strength to bear the memory.

III

I have forgotten nothing, nothing lost.
The wealth is garnered and the guard is true.
I but unlatch the gate and follow through
The haunts of memory—Oh, what a host!
Oh, lovely and familiar seeming ghost!—
And I am with you, with the whole of you.
Yes, I can count all, I can even woo
One all unnoticed then I now love most.
And who may he be? Him you knew full well.
He lingered longingly the summer o'er,
And in each open blossom saw an elf,
In each closed flower felt the darkness swell,
And from each autumn leaf saw the light pour
Over the earth: a sad, strange lad: myself.

IV

To dream away a Sabbath afternoon
Upon the hillside shadowing the lake
Wherein dim palaces of crystal wake
To view and stay and do not vanish soon;
And while the shadows thicken and the croon
Of weird night-spirits rises, and the break
Of silence is a thing of terror's make,
To stay and wait the coming of the moon.

And then to climb down to the loam below
Where flowers and trees breathe softly lest they mar
The weaving of the universal mood,
And the joy perish and the wonder go;
In this sweet earthly night to be a star,
Oh, this was youth and love and brotherhood.

V

The merchants never liked you when they passed.
They never stopped to gamble at the Inn.
They spurned our thresholds for the lovely sin
They followed ever, and they never cast
Their fortune with you—you the green, the vast;
Here, said they mocking, there's no gold to win,
And so they vanished with their horses' din—
The merchants never liked you till the last.
Ah, but the gypsies when the autumn came,
How they flocked in to rear their homely tent
From which the smoke soon rose familiarly.
You let them rob you even, and your name
To those strange nameless grew a wonderment.
And they stayed long with you and lovingly.

VI

O I must seek you out before I die
To prove my faith in beauty and in love.
For in you love and beauty grew. There strove
Those wondrous pulses with the sea and sky
And won their godhood. Once more I would lie
In the warm sunlight of your river grove
And feel dear unseen passionate fingers move
Over my eyelids closed, caressingly.

Then might the evil yet pass out of me,
And the dark stain of passion leave my soul;
For power and pleasure, wealth and fame, I know,
Are a vexation and a vanity.
All this is true, true love alone makes whole;
Such love as yours, Nustscha, could make me so.

VII

Long ere the soldiers trampled down your grass
The pride of princes was already yours.
It did not need the fret of man and horse
To kindle up your spirit, and the mass
Of moving flesh and steel and rock and brass
Glanced over you like summer dust. The wars
Have only broken you and the remorse
Of death chokes in your ruined mountain-pass.
Then did your morning hilltops lift with pride
When first my fathers fashioned in your fields
The altar unto Him they called Most High.
Oh, their great singing and their mighty stride.
Even your withered heart, remembering yields,
And the grass moves like phantoms rushing by.

. . . .

XIX

All vision fades, but splendor does not fail,
Though joy vanish and all her company,
And there be nothing left of it to see.
Splendor is in the grain. This lovely vale
Of rock and tree and pool and sky may pale
And fade some autumn with its greenery,

And its form totter, crumble utterly,
And scatter with some universal gale.
Yet be they spread ever so wide and free
The grain will cause the dream to come again.
And world formations out of mists will rise;
And there will be thoughts of eternity,
And hopes the heart of man will know are vain,
And tears will come, as now, into the eyes. . . .

Samuel Roth.

ONE PATH

Outside the Earthly Paradise,
   Beneath its cool high walls,
I walk the little grass-blurred path
   Where sunlight seldom falls.

I try no more the guarded gates
   That will not let me in;
I cease to wonder what the cause,
   What accident, what sin.

I walk the lonely path that's mine,
   My heart and I employ
Our solitude in songs about
   The near-by Kingdom's joy.

And once, while singing thus, we heard
   Applause and friendly cries,
And saw, high up, our happy kin,
   Love in their lovely eyes.

The path of lonely wayfaring
   Ends where I cannot tell:
Outside the Earthly Paradise
   I know—but that is well.

                William Alexander Percy.

THE RIVER

I came from the sunless valleys,
    And sought for the open sea,
For I thought in its gray expanses
    My peace would come to me.

I came at last to the ocean,
    And found it wild and black,
And I cried to the windless valleys,
    "Be kind and take me back!"

But the thirsty tide ran inland,
    And the salt waves drank of me,
And I who was fresh as the rainfall
    Am bitter as the sea.

Sara Teasdale.

THE CHANGELING

I met a threadbare waif below the town.
His eyes were sad, and from his dusty coat
Roses no longer crimson drooped and fell;
Pebbles which had been kisses bound his throat.

He held a cup and listlessly drank wine,
As one who knew not what he was drinking of.
And when I asked his name he answered low:
"My name is Habit—once they called me Love."

Agnes Lee.

THREE GIRLS

Three school girls pass this way each day.
Two of them go in the fluttery way
Of girls, with all that girlhood buys;
But one goes with a dream in her eyes.

Two of them have the eyes of girls
Whose hair is learning scorn of curls,
But the eyes of one are like wide doors
Opening out on misted shores.

And they will go as they go to-day
On to the end of life's short way;
Two will have what living buys,
And one will have the dream in her eyes.

Two will die as many must,
And fitly dust will welcome dust;
But dust has nothing to do with one—
She dies as soon as her dream is done.

Hazel Hall.

FROM A STREET CORNER

Like snails I see the people go
Along the pavement, row on row;
And each one on his shoulder bears
His coiling shell of petty cares—
The spiral of his own affairs.

Some peer about, some creep on blind,
But not one leaves his shell behind.
And I, who think I see so well,
Peer at the rest, but cannot tell
How much is cut off by my shell.

Eleanor Hammond.

RICHARD CORY

Whenever Richard Cory went down town,
We people on the pavement looked at him;
He was a gentleman from sole to crown,
Clean favored, and imperially slim.

And he was always quietly arrayed,
And he was always human when he talked;
But still he fluttered pulses when he said
"Good-morning," and he glittered when he walked.

And he was rich,—yes, richer than a king,—
And admirably schooled in every grace:
In fine, we thought that he was everything
To make us wish that we were in his place.

So on we worked, and waited for the light,
And went without the meat, and cursed the bread;
And Richard Cory, one calm summer night,
Went home and put a bullet through his head.

Edwin Arlington Robinson.

SHE WALKS SERENE

She walks serene, so calm and unafraid,
Her head held high, her vision straining through
The clouds which seem to hang 'twixt her and you.
New hope is in her light elastic tread,
Her soul shines through her eyes as if it fed
On heavenly food, sweet manna wet with dew,
Which morning's rosy dawn brings fresh and new.
And ever and again her feet are led
By devious ways and steep, where stumbling souls
Less strong must fall and all unheeded lie;
And I who know that through the bitter night
Her broken heart is torn, her spirit rolls
And mourns in grief because you are not nigh,
I bow my head before her glorious fight.

Virginia Taylor McCormick.

COURAGE

Because my joy is less than joy,
  My sorrow more than pain,
I mock the grief that begs for tears
  With laughter and disdain.

I hold the sunlight in my hands
  And hurl it to destroy,
Because my pain is more than pain,
  My laughter less than joy.

When I was young with happiness
  I played at being sad,
The tears I used to mock my joy
  Were all the grief I had.

I do not play at sorrow now,
  Nor shall I weep again—
But I shall smile with less than joy,
  And laugh with more than pain.

Helen Frazee-Bower.

DREAMERS

Is it a dream that we are different?
Can it be true we are the same as they—
Those beasts forever tearing at their prey,
Seeming so sleek yet always on the scent?
Our talons hide in pale pear blossom flesh,
Cold cunning lurks beneath our fragile skin,
Oh we are strange and terrible within—
Our slender hands can lay a snaring mesh!
Still, do beasts hold hushed visions as they go,
By toiling sweat do they stretch towers high—
Aching to wring a solace from the sky,
And crying of a High White Thing they know!
Are we mere beasts and cruel as we seem,
Or are we different because we dream?

Power Dalton.

THE NIGHT ARMIES

The street is gray with rain,
    The gutters run surcharged. All night
I heard war-chariots sweep the plain
    In one long-rolling wave of fight.

Now it is dawn, and I can see
    No battle wreck, no littered plain:
Where do wild night-armies flee?—
    The street is gray with rain.

And down the street an ash-cart jolts
    Ponderous, and I turn away . . .
God, how the ghost in man revolts
    Against the day!

                    Lee Wilson Dodd.

BALLAD OF THE DEAD KING

The dead King lay in his stately hall;
  The guard paced slow, paced slow;
The stars shone in at the shuttered port,
  The candles fluttered low.

Sore wearied was the sleeping King,
  With all his kingdom's care.
His face was like a winter's day—
  The snow was in his hair.

The candles threw a broken light
  About his resting-place,
And all the stillnesses of earth
  Were gathered in his face.

It seemed he came a distant way
  Through harsh, unfriendly lands,
And laid his labor at God's feet,
  And slept with folded hands.

. . . .

Across the wall where life began
  Men stopped and praised the King;
And Some One hauled the banners down,
  And made the bells to ring.

106

And Some One said the King was good,
  And Some One wept aloud,
And Some One labored night and day
  To make the King his shroud.

But little Carl, the weaver's son,
  Who played beneath the wall,
He laughed, as only childhood laughs,
  And tossed his bright new ball.

"He gave me this, the tall, gray man,"
  Thus Seven-Summers sang;
And still they hauled the banners down,
  And still the dull bells rang.

"He stopped as he went riding by,
  And bought my ball for me."
The childish laughter shrilled and died,
  The bells tolled ceaselessly.

. . . .

The dead King lay in the Halls of State,
  The guard paced slow, paced slow;
The dawn came in at the shuttered port,
  And the candles flickered low.

Sore wearied was the sleeping King
  With all his kingdom's care,
His face was like a winter's day—
  The snow was in his hair.

They bore him down at break o' day
  And laid him in his place;
And all the stillness of the tomb
  Was gathered in his face.

They sang his name in chanted psalms,
  They praised him, being dead;
Their grief was like a wind of tears—
  "He was the King!" they said.

Then high above the sobbing wind
  All suddenly there came
The tribute of the Secret Deed
  That had no thought of fame.

Shrill, shrill it rose above the crowd,
  The fairest praise of all—
The laughter of a little child
  Who played beneath the wall.

Dana Burnet.

SUCCESS

He who would rear a palace for his pride
   Oft feasted in its halls, though none remain.
Who dreamed to lift to God a perfect fane
Sculptured one deathless pillar ere he died.

Katherine Lee Bates.

HOW SWIFTLY THE BRIGHT COINS OF THOUGHT

How swiftly the bright coins of thought
Come from the busy mint, the brain,
To markets where our lives are bought—
The sense's ease, the spirit's pain.
And one will save, and one will spend,
And one, on meeting with a friend,
Some lesser coin will toss and spin
For chance of what its fall may win.

So I have tossed and spun, and held
The bright coin in my hand, to read
Whether it was a song it spelled
Or those dark fears that sorrows breed.
The elder gods all played at chance—
Thus came adventure and romance.
Our lives are shillings, like as not,
The gods have spun—and then forgot.

Amory Hare.

THE KINGS ARE PASSING DEATHWARD

The kings are passing deathward in the dark
  Of days that had been splendid where they went;
Their crowns are captive and their courts are stark
  Of purples that are ruinous, now, and rent.
For all that they have seen disastrous things:
  The shattered pomp, the split and shaken throne,
They cannot quite forget the way of Kings:
  Gravely they pass, majestic and alone.

With thunder on their brows, their faces set
  Toward the eternal night of restless shapes,
They walk in awful splendor, regal yet,
  Wearing their crimes like rich and kingly
      capes . . .
Curse them or taunt, they will not hear or see;
The Kings are passing deathward: let them be.

David Morton.

THE NIGHT OF GODS

Their mouths have drunken Death's eternal wine—
The draught that Baal in oblivion sips.
Unseen about their courts the adder slips,
Unheard the sucklings of the leopard whine;
The toad has found a resting-place divine,
And bloats in stupor between Ammon's lips.
O Carthage and the unreturning ships,
The falling pinnacle, the shifting Sign!

Lo! when I hear from voiceless court and fane
Time's adoration of Eternity—
The cry of kingdoms past and gods undone—
I stand as one whose feet at noontide gain
A lonely shore; who feels his soul set free,
And hears the blind sea chanting to the sun.

George Sterling.

NAPOLEON IN HADES

They stirred uneasily, drew down their capes,
    And whispered each to each in awed surprise,
Seeing this figure brood along the shapes,
    World tragedies thick-crowding through his eyes.
On either side the ghostly groups drew back
    In huddled knots, yielding him way and room,
Their foolish mouths agape and fallen slack,
    Their bloodless fingers pointing through the gloom.

Still lonely and magnificent in guilt,
    Splendid in scorn, wrapt in a cloudy dream,
He paused at last upon the Stygian silt,
    And raised calm eyes above the angry stream . . .
Hand in his breast, he stood till Charon came,
While Hades hummed with gossip of his name.

David Morton.

113

ULYSSES

Whole days he sits and muses by the fire,
With a full flagon and an ancient hound
Twitching in sleep beside his chair; no sound
Rouses the weary eyes, the hands that tire,
But when at even Telemachus and men
Come thundering from the hunt, with noise of
        spears,
And shields that ring upon the court, he hears,
Takes up his sword, and is himself again.

Long afternoons he paces by the shore,
And fights anew old wars and old regrets;
And where the humble fisher mends his nets,
He sees the heroes that he loved of yore.
Waiting, he stands to hail in the dim light
One proud ship more, and sail out in the night.

Beulah May.

SONNET

(From "The Middle Years")

This is the burden of the middle years:
To know what things can be, or not be, known;
To find no sunset lovely unto tears;
To pass not with the swallow southward-flown
Toward far Hesperides where gold seas break
Beyond the last horizon round strange isles;
To have forgot Prometheus on his peak;
To know that pilgrim-miles are only miles.
Then death seems not so dreadful with its night
That keeps unstirred a veil of mystery.
Then no acclaimed disaster can affright
Him who is wise in human history
And finds no godhead there to earn his praise
And dreads no horror save his empty days.

Arthur Davison Ficke.

THE UNKNOWN GREAT

Not to the brave upon the battlefield
Alone, the palms of victory belong,
Not only to the great of earth the song
Of praise and pæan should the singer yield.
Greater the souls who, single-handed, wield
The battle-axe against the hosts of wrong,
Unknown, unnoted in life's reckless throng,
And only in God's day to stand revealed.

Ah, by our side, in patient, humble guise,
How many walk the silent conqueror's way!—
As fixëd stars in fame's eternal skies
Their stainless luster worthiest to shine.
Unlaureled heroes! reverently I lay
Low at your feet this tribute leaf of mine.

Ina Coolbrith.

THE SINGER OF ONE SONG

He sang one song and died—no more but that:
A single song and carelessly complete.
He would not bind and thresh his chance-grown
       wheat,
Nor bring his wild fruit to the common vat,
To store the acid rinsings, thin and flat,
Squeezed from the press or trodden under feet.
A few slow beads, blood-red and honey-sweet,
Oozed from the grape, which burst and spilled its
       fat.

But Time, who soonest drops the heaviest things
That weigh his pack, will carry diamonds long.
So through the poet's orchestra, which weaves
One music from a thousand stops and strings,
Pierces the note of that immortal song:—
"High over all the lonely bugle grieves."

Henry A. Beers.

POETS

Heralds of joy, they walk the path of sorrow;
Bearers of light, they tread a darkened way;
Of gold bereft, from heaven's wealth they borrow;
They die in night whose souls are full of day.

Thomas Curtis Clark.

TO SONG

Here shall remain all tears for lovely things
And here enshrined the longing of great hearts,
Caught on a lyre whence waking wonder starts,
To mount afar upon immortal wings;
Here shall be treasured tender wonderings,
The faintest whisper that the soul imparts,
All silent secrets and all gracious arts
Where nature murmurs of her hidden springs.

O magic of a song! here loveliness
May sleep unhindered of life's mortal toll,
And noble things stand towering o'er the tide;
Here mid the years, untouched by time or stress,
Shall sweep on every wind that stirs the soul
The music of a voice that never died!

Thomas S. Jones, Jr.

MIRACLE

Who is in love with loveliness,
    Need not shake with cold;
For he may tear a star in two,
    And frock himself in gold.

Who holds her first within his heart,
    In certain favor goes;
If his roof tumbles, he may find
    Harbor in a rose.

Lizette Woodworth Reese.

THEY WENT FORTH TO BATTLE, BUT THEY ALWAYS FELL

They went forth to battle, but they always fell;
   Their eyes were fixed above the sullen shields;
Nobly they fought and bravely, but not well,
And sank heart-wounded by a subtle spell.
   They knew not fear that to the foeman yields,
   They were not weak, as one who vainly wields
A futile weapon; yet the sad scrolls tell
How on the hard-fought field they always fell.

It was a secret music that they heard,
   A sad sweet plea for pity and for peace;
And that which pierced the heart was but a word,
Though the white breast was red-lipped where the
     sword
   Pressed a fierce cruel kiss, to put surcease
   On its hot thirst, but drank a hot increase.
Ah, they by some strange troubling doubt were
     stirred,
And died for hearing what no foeman heard.

They went forth to battle, but they always fell;
   Their might was not the might of lifted spears;
Over the battle-clamor came a spell
Of troubling music, and they fought not well.
   Their wreaths are willows, and their tribute,
     tears;
   Their names are old sad stories in men's ears;
Yet they will scatter the red hordes of Hell,
Who went to battle forth and always fell.

Shaemas O'Sheel.

WARRIORS OF THE DREAM

They pushed their glowing joys aside,
  They laid their shining hopes away;
They hearkened, pale and starry-eyed,
  And closed the books and dropped the play.
They said, "There is a greater thing
Than fame or golden harvesting.
Out of the storm there came a cry
And we will answer, though we die!"

They answered from the seething plain,
They answered from the reeling height,
To the last reaching-forth, in pain,
They sent their answer down the night:
        "Though hope allure and love enthrall
          And precious, youth and glory seem,
        Sweeter than all, greater than all
          Is to give all to a dream!"

They will not come again to play
The old games through the summer day,
Or seek the cool woods or the brooks
Or open now the dusty books.
Yet, where in crowds, with restless feet,
The getters and the spenders meet,

There is, at times, a strange deep sound
Not from the sky, not from the ground,
And voices such as music hath
That shakes the heart and chokes the breath:
>"Though hope allure and love enthrall
>>And precious, youth and glory seem,
>Sweeter than all, greater than all
>>Is to give all to a dream!"

On its old orbit swings this earth;
   Day comes, night comes; the seasons pass;
And holy memories, amid mirth,
   Are but as shadows on a glass.
Men may forget and Time erase
Of name and deed the last faint trace;
But in still hours, amid their joys
Unborn, undreamed of girls and boys
Shall of a sudden be aware
Of something not of earth or air,
A burning brow, a glowing eye,
A flame, a presence and a cry:
>"Though hope allure and love enthrall
>>And precious, youth and glory seem,
>Sweeter than all, greater than all
>>Is to give all to a dream!"

Hermann Hagedorn.

SHELLEY

Knight-Errant of the Never-ending Quest,
And minstrel of the Unfulfilled Desire;
Forever tuning thy frail earthly lyre
To some unearthly music, and possessed
With painful passionate longing to invest
The golden dream of Love's immortal fire
With mortal robes of beautiful attire,
And fold perfection to thy throbbing breast!
What wonder, Shelley, that the restless wave
Should claim thee and the leaping flame consume
Thy drifted form on Viareggio's beach?
These were thine elements,—thy fitting grave.
But still thy soul rides on with fiery plume,
Thy wild song rings in ocean's yearning speech!

Henry van Dyke.

Who is this, of all our voices hushed beyond the
        singing shore,
Where the foamless roll of silence cradles peace for-
        evermore,
    Who is this, that still returning, mourns his eerie
        dream of Aden,
And his mystic, bloodless music chants the spell
        of lost Lenore?

Was thy singing ever mortal, warmed by human,
        fierce desires,
Ere the living passion flickered into pale, sepul-
        chral fires?
    Or was life to thee but shadow,—song to thee but
        friendless yearning,
Thy first home the spirit vision whither still thy
        heart aspires?

O thy high and pallid singing, fugitive from baf-
        fled death,
Surely moves from phantom lips, and pulses with
        unearthly breath!
    Not of earth thou wert, dead singer,—thee hath
        also death rejected?
Hath nor death nor life its laurel for thy song's
        ethereal wreath?

Changeling of the Muses, bearing mortal exile all
thy days,
Rapt from starry heights of faery to endure earth's
heavy ways,
Alien from what land, and pilgrim to what
shrine—here lost and lonely?
Even praise of thee will falter; scarce we know the
man we praise.

Lost indeed and hither fallen, as the proud light-
bearer fell,
Out of harmonies eternal, out of peace ineffable,
Into discord, into darkness, into bitterness in-
fernal,—
For to wear our wingless vesture, for a soul like
thine was hell.

Shadow-lover, building twilight-worlds of swift-
enfolding doom,
Where the haunted soul is mirrored in its own
demonic gloom,
Yet from utter darkness kindling still the tragic
flame of beauty,
Till from death, from hate, from horror streams
its melancholy bloom;

Dreamer of the dauntless will, that darkened soars
to perfect sight,
Dauntless, though this muddy garment weigh its
wings and dull its flight,
Up from lesser gloom to lesser gloom a finer ether
winning,
Till the thought escape the body into skies of cloud-
less light;

126

Shall we call thee lost, dead poet,—we whose fate
    is kin to thine?
Shadows are our world, and phantom half the stars
    that o'er us shine;
  Shall we call him lost, who faithful toward the
    light of beauty beacons,
And our days his mystic singing floods with loveli-
    ness divine?

John Erskine.

THE GARDEN OF SORROW

(Suggested by Poe Cottage, Fordham)

A mist broods over all—I gaze with love
And lingering sadness on a place I know
Too well for words; the little house where Poe
Suffered and sang. Oh, happy sky above,
Bend with a little greyness! Glad World, move
Less lightly! Here dwelt one whom darkest woe
Wrapped in unending night, and doomed to go
Where the gaunt raven rends the stricken dove.

But I alone am sad. The clean, cool skies
Are fresh with tranquil gladness . . . Vagrant flow-
     ers
Dance in the wind . . . Children at play give cries
Of joy. Ah well! perchance he, too, had hours
When Spring and childhood raised his burdened
     eyes
And blue skies brightened melancholy bowers.

Hugh Wilgus Ramsaur.

SHAKESPEARE

Because, the singer of an age, he sang
   The passions of the ages,
It was humanity itself that leaped
   To life upon his pages.

He told no single being's tale—he forced
   All beings to his pen.
And when he made a man to walk the street
   Forth walked a million men.

Agnes Lee.

THE SKULL OF SHAKESPEARE

Within how small, without how strangely vast!
What stars of terror had their path in thee!
What music of the heavens and the sea
Lived in a sigh or thundered in the blast!
Here swept the gleam and pageant of the Past,
As beauty trembled to her fate's decree;
Here swords were forged for armies yet to be,
And tears were found too dreadful not to last.

Here stood the seats of judgment and its light,
To whose assizes all our dreams were led—
Our best and worst, our Paradise and Hell;
And in this room delivered now to night,
The mortal put its question to the dead,
And worlds were weighed, and God's deep shadow
    fell.

George Sterling.

PERSEPHONE

The hour draweth near
When thou, Persephone, shalt reappear
From the mysterious realms of the dear dead
By vanished joy, lost beauty, tenanted.
The robins sing to call thee from the ground,
The maples' ruddy tresses are unbound,
The ice-locked rivers melt and gladly run
Like happy children laughing in the sun.

O bright, illusive maid,
In the dim regions where thou wast betrayed,
Tell me if thou hast met a lady dear,
Grown weary of the lengthening shadows here?
She wore a little bonnet, silk and lace,
With roses round the circle of her face,
And hearts awoke to joy where'er she trod
Because her life expressed the love of God.

I do forget! To thee
She went arrayed in regal panoply.
No little bonnet set with roses sweet,
But dressed as for her king, from head to feet
All stately grace, bedecked with lilies, fair

131

And white as was her hair.
Oh, she was very, very dear to me!
Pray has thou seen her there, Persephone?
This is the happy season of her birth.
With thy return to earth,
Canst thou not lead her gently by the hand
Back to the sunshine of her native land?—
Thou who dost in thy verdant mantle bring
The myriad flowers of immortal spring.
Dearer than any flowers beneath the skies,
The tenderness within her loving eyes.

Persephone, why tread
Through the vast, ageless regions of the dead,
Bringing the bloom of flower, the song of bird,
But from the vanished lips no loving word?
Their vaunted power the gods have lost; I know
Where they have journeyed, they we sorrow so;—
Beyond the reach of thee or thy caress,
Beyond thy jocund smile of tenderness,
Beyond thy power to woo or to retrieve,
Deep in a heart of love they would not leave.

Blithe goddess of the spring,
Persephone, we hear thy robins sing
In the long twilights that she loved to see,
When her exuberant spirit watched for thee.
Thou wilt not find her in thy somber land,
Whose outward-leading paths none understand.
Bring back thy daffodil and violet;
Upon the heavenly heights her feet are set.
Thy shadow-silences the soul must dare,
To gain the sunlight of that world more fair.

Persephone, return,
Bearing to man thine overbrimming urn;
And walk our earth as for uncounted years,
Leading coy April, clad in smiles and tears;
Woo from the underworld the laggard spring.

Our dead thou canst not bring.
My lady sees the asphodel; the rose
Of souls grown sanctified and blest she knows.
Beyond the shadow-realm the dear home-land
Waits in the loving hollow of God's hand.
She has gone far beyond thy call and cry,
Where stretch the mystic pastures of the sky,
And thou, Persephone, hast grown more fair
Because she passed thy gate in journeying there.

Edith Willis Linn.

HELEN IN HADES

All that I sought was peace and happiness,
But there was something fatal in my eyes
And maddening in my mouth; Men grew unwise
And crazed, beholding me, and Law was less
Than their desire; one vagrant, windy tress,
Or my unguarded bosom's rich surprise
Filled each man's heart with visions and vain cries
And his arms rose in dreams for my caress.

Yea, I saw neither happiness nor peace
But hungry faces bright as swords and spears;
I was the White, Unwilling Storm of Greece;
Tumult tossed round me, rising with the years . . .
What was that pale boy's name the gossips set
By mine? . . . we dead so easily forget!

Harry Kemp.

THERMOPYLÆ

Men lied to them and so they went to die.
Some fell, unknowing that they were deceived,
And some escaped, and bitterly bereaved,
Beheld the truth they loved shrink to a lie.
And those there were that never had believed,
But from afar had read the gathering sky,
And darkly wrapt in that dread prophecy,
Died trusting that their truth might be retrieved.

It matters not. For life deals thus with Man;
To die alone deceived or with the mass,
Or disillusioned to complete his span.
Thermopylæ or Golgotha, all one,
The young dead legions in the narrow pass;
The stark black cross against the setting sun.

Robert Hillyer.

The moon, a sweeping scimitar, dipped in the
    stormy straits;
The dawn, a crimson cataract, burst through the
    eastern gates,
The cliffs were robed in scarlet, the sands were
    cinnibar,
Where first two men spread wings for flight and
    dared the hawk afar.

There stands the cunning workman, the craftiest
    past all praise,
The man who chained the Minotaur, the man who
    built the Maze;
His young son is beside him, and the boy's face is
    a light,
A light of dawn and wonder and of valor infinite.

Their great vans beat the cloven air, like eagles
    they mount up,
Motes in the wine of morning, specks in a crystal
    cup,
And lest his wings should melt apace, old Dædalus
    flies low,
But Icarus beats up, beats up—he goes where light-
    nings go.

He cares no more for warnings, he rushes through
    the sky,
Braving the crags of ether, daring the gods on high,
Black 'gainst the crimson sunset, golden o'er cloudy
    snows,
With all Adventure in his heart, the first winged
    man arose.

Dropping gold, dropping gold, where the mists of
    morning rolled,
On he kept his way undaunted, though his breaths
    were stabs of cold,
Through the mystery of dawning that no mortal
    may behold.

Now he shouts, now he sings in the rapture of his
    wings,
And his great heart burns intenser with the strength
    of his desire,
As he circles like a swallow, wheeling, flaming, gyre
    on gyre.

Gazing straight at the sun, half his pilgrimage is
    done,
And he staggers for a moment, hurries on, reels
    backward, swerves
In a rain of scattered feathers, as he falls in broken
    curves!

Icarus, Icarus, though the end is piteous,
Yet forever, yea, forever, we shall see thee rising
    thus,
See the first supernal glory, not the ruin hideous.

You were man; you who ran farther than our eyes
     can scan,
Man, absurd, gigantic, eager for impossible ro-
     mance,
Overthrowing all Hell's legions with one warped and
     broken lance!

On the highest steeps of space he will have his
     dwelling place;
In those far, terrific regions where the cold comes
     down like Death
Gleams the red glint of his pinions, smoke, the
     vapor of his breath.
Floating downward very clear, still the echoes reach
     the ear
Of a little tune he whistles and a little song he
     sings,
Mounting, mounting still, triumphant, on his torn
     and broken wings!

Stephen Vincent Benét.

THE SCHOOL BOY READS HIS ILIAD

The sounding battles leave him nodding still:
  The din of javelins at the distant wall
Is far too faint to wake that weary will
  That all but sleeps for cities where they fall.
He cares not if this Helen's face were fair,
  Nor if the thousand ships shall go or stay;
In vain the rumbling chariots throng the air
  With sounds the centuries shall not hush away.

Beyond the window where the Spring is new,
  Are marbles in a square, and tops again,
And floating voices tell him what they do,
  Luring his thought from these long-warring
      men,—
And though the camp be visited with gods,
He dreams of marbles and of tops, and nods.

David Morton.

WHAT IF THE LAPSE OF AGES WERE A DREAM?

What if the lapse of ages were a dream,
From which we waked, clutching the primal bough,
Seeing familiar thunder-piercing crags,
Vast dripping woods, and saurian-bellowed swamps,
That wearied the new heavens with their noise,
Wild seas, that maddened, foaming, ever gnawed
At fog-wrapped cliffs, and roaring in defeat,
Ran to eye-wearying distance, without shore—
All things familiar; but our dull ape minds
Troubled with visions vague; the hungry roar
Of the great sabred tiger far below
Seeming in our wild dream the thund'rous sound
Of hurtling heated monsters, made of steel;
And the God-scattered worlds that gem the sky
Seeming in vision dread the blinding glare
Of myriad windows in huge range on range
Of mountain buildings, teeming o'er with life.
The wallowing pleiosaurus' gurgling snort
Changed in our dream to rhythmic, panting roar
Of black, insensate steel amphibians,
Daring the ocean's dread horizon line;
And the high flap of pterodactyl wings
Making us whine with fear, for, in our dream,
We saw vast lifeless birds, that roaring flew,
Commanded by weak puny likenesses
Of our ape-selves; we cringed with terrors vague
Of ungrasped thoughts we could not understand—
What if the lapse of ages were a dream?

Stephen Moylan Bird.

140

TO AN INHABITANT OF PARADISE

How goes it in your star-lit world—
The silences, the brooding wood?
Does there the tiger hunt no more,
The falcon twitter for his hood?

Have you stripped all the boughs that talk
And calmed the torrents from the hill?
Are lamb and wolf now reconciled?
Is hunger banished from your sill?

Does that inexorable whip,
Which drove us heedless face to face,
No longer burn along your veins
Or cut your new dispassionate grace?

Do you watch struggle unconcerned,
Hear voices call you and not speak,
There in your timeless acres feel
Above your kinship with the weak?

Oh, guard the gates that shut you in!
Make sure the world behind your eyes!
My world of men and lust and wheels
Begins to march on Paradise.

Scudder Middleton.

ABRAHAM LINCOLN WALKS AT MIDNIGHT
In Springfield, Illinois

It is portentous, and a thing of state
That here at midnight in our little town,
A mourning figure walks, and will not rest,
Near the old court-house pacing up and down.

Or by his homestead, or in shadowed yards,
He lingers where his children used to play;
Or through the market, on the well-worn stones,
He stalks until the dawn-stars burn away.

A bronzed lank man! His suit of ancient black,
A famous high top-hat and plain worn shawl,
Make his the quaint great figure that men love,
The prairie lawyer, master of us all.

He cannot sleep upon his hillside now.
He is among us—as in times before!
And we who toss and lie awake for long
Breathe deep, and start, to see him pass the door.

His head is bowed. He thinks on men and kings.
Yea, when the sick world cries, how can he sleep?
Too many peasants fight, they know not why;
Too many homesteads in black terror weep.

142

The sins of all the war-lords burn his heart.
He sees the dreadnaughts scouring every main.
He carries on his shawl-wrapped shoulders now
The bitterness, the folly and the pain.

He cannot rest until a spirit-dawn
Shall come—the shining hope of Europe free:
The league of sober folk, the Workers' Earth,
Bringing long peace to Cornland, Alp and Sea.

It breaks his heart that kings must murder still,
That all his hours of travail here for men
Seem yet in vain. And who will bring white peace
That he may sleep upon his hill again?

Vachel Lindsay.

NOVEMBER 11, 1918

Suddenly bells and flags!
   Suddenly—door to door—
Tidings! Can we believe,
   We, who were used to war?

Yet we have dreamed of Peace,
   Knowing her light must be,
Knowing that she must come.
   Look—she comes, it is she!

Tattered her raiment floats,
   Blood is upon her wings.
Ah, but her eyes are clear!
   Ah, but her glad heart sings!

Soon where the shrapnel fell
   Petals will wake and stir.
Look—she is here, she lives!
   Beauty has died for her.

Agnes Lee.

144

THE CHASM

There is a chasm in the world, more dark
Than any carved of rivers and slow Time,
A murky horror in a frosty clime,
Where no sun peers, no pale moon's virgin arc.
There Shame and Fear, twin wolves, forever bark,
Huddling their stolen herd in night and grime,
Forsaken culprits guilty of no crime,
Gnawed, harried, crushed, heart-stricken, hopeless,
        stark.

Forever moaning Why? forever Why?
The lost ones err about the gloomy damps,
Too poor, too rich, too young, too frail to blame,
They live obscurely and obscurely die,
For these are they who have burned out their lamps
Ere yet they knew what meant the golden flame.

Hermann Hagedorn.

(Chant of the Weary Workers)

A-drift . . . Let us drift this night, let us drift on
      the river,
Herded and huddled. Our boat drifts on and on.
The dim far lights of the city shiver.
Dim in our hearts the lost lights quiver.
We are leaden and weary and wan.

Let us drift . . . let us drift, let us drift, let us
      drift forever.
A fog's in the air . . . The river is white and still.
They are gleams, they are dreams, the ships that
      are faintly passing;
They are gleams, they are dreams, that the river is
      softly glassing . . .
O city, have pity this night! All day we have bent
      to your will!

Is it thy breath, O Death, that has touched the
      city?
That has made that hard face soft, and those hard
      eyes kind?
Is it Death that has brought and taught to our
      master pity?

146

Is it thy white breath, O Death, in the heart of the
        city,
And is it a corpse and a phantom we leave behind?

Is it Death? . . . Let us drift. We are weary, too
        weary for weeping;
Too weary to labor, to love, too weary to roam.
The waters, the air and the sky, they are sleeping,
        sleeping.
Let us drift. . . . On the air a silence like sorrow
        is creeping.
We are weary of going to work. O God! We are
        weary of going home!

Edward H. Pfeiffer.

I FOUND A BEGGAR STARVING

I found a beggar starving
  In the windy street one night;
A crescent moon swung overhead
  And the houses twinkled bright.

A music fluttered to the moon,
  The houses seemed to sway;
I heard the whirl of dancing feet
  And laughter of the gay.

I found a beggar starving,
  He was a guest—he said,
But from the feast rose pallid
  Like the faint moon overhead.

"Your eyes"—I said, "stare madly,
  Your lips with cold are mute;
How can it be you hunger
  In the street of wine and fruit?"

The beggar spoke—"You wonder
  I starve with meat and drink,
While goodly bowls are steaming
  And brimming glasses clink.

148

Gold cannot feed my visions
  Nor quench my thirst of dreams,
For I am one of millions
  Who starve where living teems.

A star is rich with fire,
  How lone it crawls above—
Just like a beggar starving
  Who hungers after love!"

Morris Abel Beer.

149

AN AUGUST NIGHT IN THE CITY

I know a sad park where, on breathless nights,
Throng those whom through the day the hot sun
        smites—
The pallid poor, unlettered and alone,
Whose hearts are hotter than the aching stone.

This is their dormitory; here they fare
After the Summer noon's relentless glare.
See! here they crowd like sheep without a fold,
While all around them rings the city's gold.

But there are coasts beside a lonely sea,
And hills and glens and many a wind-swept lea
Where man has never broken the silence deep. . .
Yet here to-night an army falls asleep!

Charles Hanson Towne.

THE WALL STREET PIT

I see a hell of faces surge and whirl,
Like maelstrom in the ocean—faces lean
And fleshless as the talons of a hawk—
Hot faces like the faces of the wolves
That track the traveler fleeing through the night—
Grim faces shrunken up and fallen in,
Deep-plowed like weather-eaten bark of oak—
Drawn faces like the faces of the dead,
Grown suddenly old upon the brink of earth.

Is this a whirl of madmen ravening,
And blowing bubbles in their merriment?
Is Babel come again with shrieking crew
To eat the dust and drink the roaring wind?
And all for what? A handful of bright sand
To buy a shroud with and a length of earth?

Edwin Markham.

FIFTEEN

(To a Face on Fifth Avenue)

How close must be the city air
  To make your young head droop so soon,
Ere ever May's wild-flying hair
  Yield to the silken bonds of June!

Faded! Before the bloom, the blight!
  Unshamed, but faded! Where are now
Those tremulous glories that made bright
  That powdered cheek and brow?

Oh, cheek that flamed, oh, sparkling eyes!
  Was it for this, that perfect mirth?
For this the love, the sacrifice,
  The patience, and the pangs of birth?

Faded! And now the long decay;
  Years, and the hungering look behind.
November on the heels of May!
  A crumpled leaf, the whirling wind!

Hermann Hagedorn.

.

LILACS IN THE CITY

Amid the rush and fever of the street,
    The snarl and clash of countless quarreling bells,
And the sick, heavy heat,
    The hissing footsteps, and the hateful smells,
I found you, speaking quietly
    Of sunlit hill-horizons and clean earth;
    While the pale multitude that may not dare
To pause and live a moment, lest they die,
    Swarmed onward with hot eyes, and left you
            there—
An armful of God's glory, nothing worth.

You are more beautiful than I can know.
    Even one loving you might gaze an hour
Nor learn the perfect flow
    Of line and tint in one small, perfect flower.
There are no two of you the same,
And every one is wonderful and new—
    Poor baby-blossoms that have died unblown,
    And you that droop yourselves as if for shame,
You are too perfect. I had hardly known
    The grace of your glad sisters but for you.

You myriads of little litanies!
    Not as our bitter piety, subdued

To cold creed that denies
  Or lying law that severs glad and good;
But like a child's eyes, after sleep
  Uplifted; like a girl's first wordless prayer
  Close-held by him who loves her—no distress
Nor storm of supplication, but a deep,
  Dear heartache of such utter happiness
As only utter purity can bear.

For you are all the robin feels at dawn;
  The meaning of green dimness, and calm noons
On high fields far withdrawn,
  Where the haze glimmers and the wild bee croons.
You are the soul of a June night:—
  Intimate joy of moon-swept vale and glade,
Warm fragrance breathing upward from the ground,
  And eager winds tremulous with sharp delight
Till all the tense-tuned gloom thrills like a sound—
  Mystery of sweet passion unafraid.

O sweet, sweet, sweet! You are the proof of all
  That over-truth our dreams have memory of
That day cannot recall:
  Work without weariness, and tearless love,
And taintless laughter. While we run
To measure dust, and sounding names are hurled
  Into the nothingness of days unborn,
You hold your little hearts up to the sun,
  Quietly beautiful amid our scorn—
God's answer to the wisdom of this world.

                              Brian Hooker.

154

DAFFODILS

Fathered by March, the daffodils are here.
First, all the air grew keen with yesterday,
And once a thrush from out some hollow gray
On a field's edge, where whitening stalks made
    cheer,
Fluted the last unto the budding year;
Now, that the wind lets loose from orchard spray
Plum bloom and peach bloom down the dripping
    way,
Their punctual gold through the wet blades they
    rear.
Oh, fleet and sweet! A light to all that pass
Below, in the cramped yard, close to the street,
Long-stemmed one flames behind the palings bare,
The whole of April in a tuft of grass.
Scarce here, soon will it be—oh, sweet and fleet!—
Gone like a snatch of song upon the stair.

Lizette Woodworth Reese.

WASTED HOURS

There was a day I wasted long ago,
  Lying upon a hillside in the sun—
An April day of wind and drifting clouds,
  An idle day and all my work undone.

The little peach trees with their coral skirts
  Were dancing up the hillside in the breeze;
The grey walled meadows gleamed like bits of jade
  Against the crimson bloom of maple trees.

And I could smell the warmth of trodden grass,
  The coolness of a freshly harrowed field;
And I could hear a bluebird's wistful song
  Of love and beauty only half revealed.

I have forgotten many April days
  But one there is that comes to haunt me still—
A day of feathered trees and windy skies
  And wasted hours on a sunlit hill.

Medora Addison.

CANTICLE

Devoutly worshipping the oak,
  Wherein the barred owl stares,
The little feathered forest folk
  Are praying sleepy prayers.

Praying the summer to be long
  And drowsy to the end,
And daily full of sun and song,
  That broken hopes may mend.

Praying the golden age to stay
  Until the whip-poor-will
Appoints a windy moving day,
  And hurries from the hill.

William Griffith.

A TULIP GARDEN

Guarded within the old red wall's embrace,
Marshalled like soldiers in gay company,
The tulips stand arrayed. Here infantry
Wheels out into the sunlight. What bold grace
Sets off their tunics, white, with crimson lace!
Here are platoons of gold-frocked cavalry,
With scarlet sabres tossing in the eye
Of purple batteries, every gun in place.
Forward they come, with flaunting colors spread,
With torches burning, stepping out in time
To some quick, unheard march. Our ears are dead,
We cannot catch the tune. In pantomime
Parades that army. With our utmost powers
We hear the wind stream through a bed of flowers.

Amy Lowell.

FUGITIVE

Behind these falling curtains of the rain,
  Beauty goes by, a phantom on the hill,
A timid fugitive beyond the lane,
  In rainy silver,—and so shy and still
That only peering eyes of some hid bird,
  Or furry ears that listened by a stone,
Could guess at Something neither seen nor heard,
  Finding escape, and faring by, alone.

For eyes like ours, too faint a thing and fleet,
  Too lightly running for such ears to hear
The stealthy going of those weightless feet;
  No thrilling sight or sound of her comes near,
Only the shining grasses where they lie,
Give hint of silver slippers hasting by.

                                    David Morton.

FORGOTTEN

All day the branches are so softly stirred,
   And ever comes a song the wind has made,
   The sunlight mingles with the drowsy shade,
Deep in the wood a lonely thrush is heard.

Quiet and peace across the sleeping vale
   That was forgot so many years ago;
   Now through the pathways tall rank grasses grow,
Tossing unhindered in the gentle gale.

For they who used to walk these lovely ways
   Long since departed nor will come again—
   Never a footstep in the scented lane
That once had known such happy yesterdays.

And where the path was then so red with bloom
   Only the creeping brier its tangle shows;
   Save in the last still watches, one lone rose
Sends through the ghostly dusk a faint perfume.

And they who rest and long have found surcease
   Upon the little hill girt round with trees,
   Are silent through the seasons' mysteries,
Deep in the slumber of their simple peace.

Dear lonely place, you mean so much to me
   For I have known as you the joy of Spring,
   And somehow in your sweet remembering
You touch the very soul of memory.

Thomas S. Jones, Jr.

THE SOUND OF THE SEA

Always here where I sleep I hear the sound of the
    sea,
    Rolling along the dunes, along the desolate places,
    Full of a memory vague of dreams and remem-
        bered faces.
Always here where I sleep I hear the sound of the
    sea.

So have I heard it sound for twenty summers or
    more,
    Roaring up through the meadows between the
        illuminate houses,
    Up through the starry fields where the black herd
        sleepily browses.
So have I heard it sound for twenty summers or
    more.

Ever that sound it has, always, whenever I hear it.
    Sometimes it makes me happy, remembering
        days that were glad
    And full of the breath of June, sometimes it
        makes me sad—
Ever that sound it has, always, whenever I hear it.

Under quivering stars and stars that were clouded
and scattered,
All through my moments of joy and pain, of
sleeping and dreaming,
Always that quiet murmur sorrowfully was
streaming,
Under quivering stars and stars that were clouded
and scattered.

Out of that somber voice swept on the wings of
Time,
Shall I not, bending down from the starry trellis
of heaven,
Look on this empty room, these meadows shining
and even—
Out of that somber voice swept on the wings of
Time!

John Hall Wheelock.

The souls of the cruel, dead kings ride out on the
    wind to-night,
  They slash the trees as they pass, and the branches
    shiver and fall;
  They thunder with galloping hoofs on the roofs of
    cottage and hall,
And the flame on the hearth leaps high, and we cross
    ourselves in fright.

Kings that were slain in fury, and kings that per-
    ished in pride,
  They have bridled the black North winds and
    loosed them to work their will.
  They crash through the lowest valley, they sweep
    up the highest hill,
And the sound of a thousand trumpets goes with
    them the while they ride.

The souls of the cruel, dead kings are out in the
    hail and snow.
  (That was a mailed hand striking just now at the
    window bars)!
  I wish I might think of my placid saints or the
    friendly, vigilant stars;
But my heart is a blown and trampled leaf on the
    roads the mad kings go.

Theodosia Garrison.

DAWN BROKE TO-DAY

Dawn broke to-day, a sodden, beaten thing,
Old and forlorn and wet with tears of grief,
As though some secret violence had befallen,
Leaving Day dumb, heart-broken, quivering.
The hush of death held every flower and leaf,
Only the brooks ran turbulent and swollen.
And, strangely, in long silences that hung
Upon the air, void as a tongueless bell,
A leaf would fall, sedately and alone,
Stripped from the vibrant bough where it had clung
By some stray wind from whence no one could tell,
Drifting unhurriedly to the Unknown,
Much as old dear beliefs will fall at last
Yellowed by time, tear-wet, but still believing.
Hour after hour leaves floated down, forlorn,
And all the trees seemed dreaming of the past,
So that one could not tell if they were grieving
For beauty missed or beauty they had borne.
And presently, like drops from some heart's blood,
The slow red leaves came dripping through the air,
The smell of death, decay and soaking mud
Went floating past and settled everywhere:
The very pulses slowed, for nothing moved;
All was so old, exhausted and unloved.

Then from the stubble, swiftly, without sound,
A late lark soared and dived and disappeared:
And all was changed—the seamed and wrinkled
    ground
Became an old face memory has endeared;
A clownish wind leapt up, and in a trice
The sober trees with gusty laughter shook;
The fallen leaves ran past like little mice;
A patch of ragged blue shone in the brook;
And in the blind and darkened soul of me,
Brightly as flags, my thoughts flew gallantly.

Amory Hare.

WIND AND LYRE

Thou art the wind and I the lyre:
   Strike, O Wind, on the sleeping strings—
   Strike till the dead heart stirs and sings!
I am the altar and thou the fire:
   Burn, O Fire, to a snowy flame—
   Burn me clean of the mortal blame!

I am the night and thou the dream:
   Touch me softly and thrill me deep,
   When all is white on the hills of sleep.
Thou art the moon and I the stream:
   Shine to the trembling heart of me,
   Light my soul to the mother-sea.

Edwin Markham.

AUTUMN SONG

Once more the crimson rumor
    Fills the forest and the town;
And the green fires of summer
    Are burning, burning down.

Oh, the green fires of summer
    Are burning down once more!
And my heart is in the ashes
    On the forest floor.

William Griffith.

Said a rose amid the June night to a little wind
there walking
(And the whisper of the moonlight was no fainter
than its talking):
"It is plainly providential," so remarked the garden
Tory,
"That the ultimate essential is the gentle rose's
glory.
Let the sordid delvers cavil! Through the world-
fog sinking seaward
And the planetary travail God was slowly groping
me-ward.
Weary ages of designing, æons of creative throes
Spent the Master in refining sullen chaos to a rose!
Shall He robe His chosen meanly? Look upon me;
am I splendid?"
Here she stood erect and queenly, curled a lip and
ended.
And the little wind there walking, not desirous of
dissension,
In a gust of cryptic talking freely granted the
contention.

Like the murmur of a far stream or a zephyr in the
sedges,

168

Scarcely louder than the star-gleam raining silver
 on the hedges,
Came a whisper from the humus where the roots
 were toiling blindly:
"They enslave us, they entomb us! Is it just and
 is it kindly?
Ours, forever ours, to nourish—oh, the drear, eternal
 duty!—
That the idle rose may flourish in aristocratic
 beauty.
Not for us the wooing, tender moon emerges from
 the far night;
Not for us the morning splendor and the witchery
 of starlight;
Not for us the dulcet cantion of the rain to throb-
 bing lutes
And there's no cerulean mansion for the roots."
Now the little wind, demurely sympathetic, cogi-
 tated,
And declared the matter surely ought to be investi-
 gated.

"Fie!" observed the fair patrician, "on their silly
 martyr poses!
Not content with their condition, always wanting to
 be roses!"
Whereupon a theophanic, superlunar phosphores-
 cense
Flung the haughty into panic, awed the humble to
 quiescence.
'Twas the Vintner of the June-wind on his world-
 wide, endless vagrance;

And he spoke the tongue of moonshine in the dialect
  of fragrance:
"Brother, Sister, softly, softly! Glooming, gleam-
  ing though the way be,
Who is low and who is lofty in the scheme of what
  you may be?
Pride and plaint are irreligious. Root and blossom,
  lo! you plod
Upward to some far, prodigious rose of God!"
And the little wind, though shyly sleeping out the
  time of talking,
Woke to praise the sermon highly, and continued
  with his walking.

John G. Neihardt.

BALLADE OF THE DREAMLAND ROSE

Where the waves of burning cloud are rolled
  On the further shore of the sunset sea,
In a land of wonder that none behold,
  There blooms a rose on the Dreamland Tree
That stands in the Garden of Mystery
  Where the River of Slumber softly flows;
And whenever a dream has come to be,
  A petal falls from the Dreamland Rose.

In the heart of the tree, on a branch of gold,
  A silvern bird sings endlessly
A mystic song that is ages old,
  A mournful song in a minor key,
Full of the glamour of faëry;
  And whenever a dreamer's ears unclose
To the sound of that distant melody,
  A petal falls from the Dreamland Rose.

Dreams and visions in hosts untold
  Throng around on that moonlit lea:
Dreams of age that are calm and cold,
  Dreams of youth that are fair and free—
Dark with a lone heart's agony,
  Bright with a hope that no one knows—
And whenever a dream and a dream agree,
  A petal falls from the Dreamland Rose.

171

Envoi

Princess, you gaze in a reverie
  Where the drowsy firelight redly glows;
Slowly you raise your eyes to me . . .
  A petal falls from the Dreamland Rose.

Brian Hooker.

"SHE WANDERED AFTER STRANGE GODS . . ."

O have you seen my fairy steed?
  His eyes are wild, his mane is white,
He feeds upon an elfin weed
  In cool of autumn night.

O have you heard my fairy steed,
  Whose cry is like a wandering loon?
He mourns some cloudy star-strewn mead
  On mountains of the moon.

O have you tamed my fairy horse
  To mount upon his back and ride?
He tears the great trees in his course,
  Nor ever turns aside.

'Tis he who tames a fairy thing
  Must suffer want and bitter fate!
Deftly the bridles did I fling
  That brought him to my gate.

I soothed and fed and tendered him
  Sweet herbs and honey in a cup,
And led him in the twilight dim
  To where a spring welled up.

But there his wings they waved so bright
  Before my eyes, I drooped and slept.
When I awoke, it seemed dark night.
  I raised my voice and wept.

Alas, my lightsome fairy steed!
  I saw my pastures trampled bare
Where I had sown the springtime seed
  And planted flowers rare!

I saw my barns a mass of flame!
  His fiery wings had glanced in flight.
And me—a prey to fear and shame—
  He left, to seek the light!

Laura Benét.

ALLEGORY

There is a temple in our mystic city
Where mumbling masks perpetually come.
The mightly gates are brass. Two women stand,
Two brazen figures, veiled and vast and dumb,
Beside the doors like sentinels on each hand,
And one is Fear, and one—alas!—is Pity.

Without those speechless courts, that awful portal,
The light of sun or star is never known:
Dim pillars rise and some strange altar fire
Burns gem-like in the dark where shadows moan,
And hollow echoes as of bells are dire,
And mockery flouts the path of every mortal.

There, from the velvet walls drip down confusion,
Mixings of soul and sense, of shadow and sound
Which on the spirit fall like blood and rain.
I think the place is some enchanted ground
Where kneeling masks implore eternal pain
Of their mad god whose name is Disillusion!

My soul, my love and I came here one day,
And wondered at the walls, the fire, the floors,
The drip of silence and the lisping dead,
And all we knelt by vague, mysterious doors—
Then horror fell upon us and we fled,
My love and I. My soul remained to pray.

Howard Mumford Jones.

THE TIGER-WOMAN

The Tiger-Woman came to me
When dusk was close and men were dull.
She beckoned from the jungle-path.
I followed, dreaming, fanciful.

The Tiger-Woman's face is pale,
But oh, her speaking eyes are dark.
No beast can move so lithe as she
Beside the matted river's mark.

The jungle is a fearsome place
For men who hunt and men who slay,
But I was not afraid to go
Where Tiger-Woman led the way.

The Tiger-Woman's lips are thin.
Her teeth are like the Tiger's teeth.
Yet her soft hands are woman's hands
And oh, the warm blood beats beneath.

She led me to a little glade—
The creepers with the moon inwove—
And two great stripèd beasts leapt up
And fawned upon her breast in love.

176

The Tiger-Woman's voice was sweet;
I hearkened and was not afraid.
She stroked the Tiger's fearful jaws;
Upon their heads my hands I laid.

And all the jungle things drew near,
And all the leaves a music made,
Like spirits chaunting in a choir
Along the bamboo colonnade.

Too sweet for human harps to sound,
It touched my blood; it fired my heart.
The Tiger-Woman sang, and I
Sang too, and understood her art.

The moon rose up as never yet
A moon of love had blessed the air.
Oh, give my breast the Tiger's heart
To tame me and to keep me there.

Donald Davidson.

MADMAN'S SONG

Better to see your cheek grown hollow,
　Better to see your temple worn,
Than to forget to follow, follow,
　After the sound of a silver horn.

Better to bind your brow with willow
　And follow, follow until you die
Than to sleep with your head on a golden pillow,
　Nor lift it up when the hunt goes by.

Better to see your cheek grown sallow
　And your hair grown gray, so soon, so soon,
Than to forget to hallo, hallo,
　After the milk-white hounds of the moon.

Elinor Wylie.

178

IMPROVIDENT

"And I shall sing a song," I said,
  "Or sit upon a hill
To watch the April breezes tease
  The freshet by the mill.

"A primrose chaplet I shall wear,
  And place upon my hair,
Then run the fields the livelong day,
  Nor give a thought to care."

This did I even as I sang
  And danced the glades along,
But soon the primrose wreath was dead,
  And dead was daylight's song.

"It had been wiser," then said I,
  "If I had made a hood
To shelter me when darkness fell
  Upon the field and wood."

Hesper Le Gallienne.

THE FALCONER OF GOD

I flung my soul to the air like a falcon flying.
I said, "Wait on, wait on, while I ride below!
  I shall start a heron soon
  In the marsh beneath the moon—
A strange white heron rising with silver on its wings,
    Rising and crying
  Wordless, wondrous things:
The secret of the stars, of the world's heart-strings,
  The answer to their woe.
Then stoop thou upon him, and grip and hold him
    so!"

My wild soul waited on as falcons hover.
I beat the reedy fens as I trampled past.
  I heard the mournful loon
  In the marsh beneath the moon.
And then—with feathery thunder—the bird of my
    desire
    Broke from the cover
  Flashing silver fire.
High up among the stars I saw his pinions spire.
  The pale clouds gazed aghast
As my falcon stoopt upon him, and gript and held
    him fast.

My soul dropt through the air—with heavenly
 plunder?—
Gripping the dazzling bird my dreaming knew?
 Nay! but a piteous freight,
 A dark and heavy weight
Despoiled of silver plumage, its voice forever
 stilled,—
 All of the wonder
 Gone that ever filled
Its guise with glory. Oh, bird that I have killed,
 How brilliantly you flew
Across my rapturous vision when first I dreamed
 of you!

 Yet I fling my soul on high with new endeavor,
 And I ride the world below with a joyful mind.
 I shall start a heron soon
 In the marsh beneath the moon—
A wondrous silver heron its inner darkness fledges.
 I beat forever
 The fens and the sedges.
 The pledge is still the same—for all distastrous
 pledges,
 All hopes resigned!
My soul still flies above me for the quarry it shall
 find.

William Rose Benét.

THE HORSEMAN

My spirit is a horseman
  Riding, riding on,
Relentlessly, relentlessly,
  To the burst of dawn.

It rides on as the stars ride
  To that burst of light,
Forgetting, forgetting
  Stars only shine by night.

Idella Purnell.

DE GUSTIBUS

One used his pinions eagle-like,
   And straight against the sun would rise
And scout among the stars, and strike
   His quarry from across the skies;

And one was as the bee that strives
   Against no wind, but simply blows
Across the garden, and arrives
   Upon an unsuspected rose.

John Erskine.

THE FUTILE

The stone falls, the bird flies, the arrow goes home,
But we have no motion, we scatter like foam.

O, give me a song to sing for your sorrow,
A song that will lift, like a wave from the reef,
You and myself, that will fling like an arrow
My poor scattered words to the target of grief:
I want to forget, to remember no morrow,
To go with the petrel, to go with the leaf. . . .

We would fly with all things to the goal of their
    flying,
We would turn with all things to the magnetic star,
But we never can live, because of our dying,
And we never can be, for the things that we are.

We alone of all creatures—the stones more than
    we—
Have no end, no motion, no destiny.

Genevieve Taggard.

THE PLAY

And still the play goes on, nor ever palls—
   Laughter and comedy and mock despair;
But nightly, as the final curtain falls,
   Mirth doffs her mask to show the face of Care.

Doris Kenyon.

Out of the Dusk they troop, my son, from the utter-
    most pales of the Past,
Where the spark of their lives was lit by the Norns
    and their courses molded and cast.
As a cavalcade they ride them forth, in a line from
    Ab to you;
Your brawn is theirs and your brain is theirs; you
    do as they bid you do.
The urge of a million sires and dames in the blood
    of your pulses runs
As your own urge will sometime surge in the sons
    of your children's sons.
In weird array the grim and gay, the priest and the
    pagan ride;
The knight with the knave, the king with the slave
    and the wanton, side by side.
Out of the dusk they troop—a wild, fantastical
    masque of man,
As we shall ride in the blood of our sons in the
    phantom caravan.

. . . .

    The Pilgrim with the Vandal rides,
      The Saxon with the Gaul,
    The sons of David, Lludd and Noah
      Ride with the sons of Saul.

One is a Prince Henry of Navarre;
  Leonidas is there,
And Richard of the Lion Heart
  And Alex Do-and-Dare.

One is the Seigneur Ber du Lac,
  Sometimes surnamed The Lance,
Who fought the fight and died the death
  With Joan, the Maid of France.

And one is Aram, priest of Baal,
  Who braved the wrath of Tyre
To preach his Word, and for that Word
- Was done to death by fire.

And one is Arnold, he whose voice
  Nor King nor Pope could still,
Who fought for Right,—and for that Right
  Was hanged on Caelus Hill.

One is Gur Khan of Balasghun,
  The warrior King and Seer,
Who broke the might of Islam's arms
  At Ibn al-Athir.

And hosts there be of goodly folk
  Who run of small renown,—
Of soldier, merchant, scholar, prince,
  Of cobbler, clerk, and clown.

And one is Anne, who watched the herds
  And spread her humble board
Before the poor, and spun the flax
  And died within the Lord.

And there be shepherd, tradesman, groom
　Who went but lowly ways,
Who tilled the field, and ground the grain
　Through unadventured days.

And some be of the wastrel folk,
　Of spendthrift, tyrant, cheat,
Of wanton, witch, and thief, who grew
　As tares grow in the wheat.

There ride Sir Sidney, Bayard, Drake,
　There Cyrus rides, the Mede,
And some there be of Hector's line
　And some of Beowulf's breed.

These be the folk who kept the faith
　And lived and loved thereby,—
Who fought the fight, who ran the race,
　Who died as men should die.

·　·　·　·　·　·　·　·　·　·　·　·　·　·

The flames of a million sires and dames in the blood
　　of your pulses run;
Of a million flames to feed and serve, how can you
　　serve but one?
Their prides are yours; their loves and their lusts,
　　their hopes and their hates are your own;
You are the fruit that their loins have bred, the
　　flower of the seed they have sown.
Their lives are spun as the threads of your cloak,
　　through the warp and the woof of your Whole;
Your hands are theirs and your eyes are theirs and
　　your Mold and your Self and your Soul.

The dreams they dreamed and the fights they fought
    and the prayers that their lips have prayed
Shall be your dreams and shall be your prayers;
    your fights are the fights they made.
The lives they lived and the deaths they died you
    shall live and die again;
In you is the seed of a million hopes of a million
    maids and men.
God grant, my son, that you fight the fight and hold
    to the faith.   Amen!

                        Kendall Banning.

CHAMBERS OF IMAGERY

Sometimes, within the brain's old ghostly house,
I hear, far off, at some forgotten door,
A music and an eerie faint carouse,
And stir of echoes down the creaking floor,

And then I rise and through the dusty gloom
Grope with swift fingers as a blind man goes,
Half sensing, half remembering the room,
Building the image of the world he knows,

And fumbling so down lightless passages
And winding stairs and windowless dark halls,
Now beckoned by the music's faint excess,
Now lost and listening at unsounding walls,

I come at last where, bolted in the stone,
A ruined door leans inward, and beyond
The voices clamor and the tune is blown
In swirl and silence of wind-troubled sound.

And then, impassioned of the thronging gods,
Eager of beauty, unlock bolts and bars,—
Alone, with grinning head that nods and nods,
Myself stand gibbering against the stars.

Archibald MacLeish.

MEMORY

Here only echoes build a futile chime
Out of the winds that blew the broken rose,
And Life's a shadow-masque withdrawn from Time
Where Love, a crying singer, comes and goes
When moons are blowing and the earth is white
With beauty or the thought of beauty dead;
And here broods Sorrow with a hanging head,
And pale Regret moans every candle-light. . . .

George Brandon Saul.

A MEMORY

Is it the spirit of a dream—
  The dearest memory—
Is it the essence of a flower,
  The soul of ecstasy?—

As the pure fragrance that is given
  To steal upon the air,
The long-loved memory of you
  Steals on me, unaware:

And everything that's beautiful,
  And everything that's true,
And everything that's lovely, pure,
  Is in the thought of you.

Brookes More.

RECOLLECTION

I must forget awhile the mellow flutes
And all the lyric wizardry of strings;
   The fragile clarinet,
Tremulous over meadows rich with dawn,
    Must knock against my vagrant heart
    And throb and cry no more.

For I am shaken by the loveliness
And lights and laughter and beguiling song
   Of all this siren world;
The regal beauty of women, round on round,
    The swift, lithe slenderness of girls,
    And children's loyal eyes,

Hill rivers and the lilac fringe of seas
Lazily plunging, glow of city nights
   And faces in the glow—
These things have stolen my heart away, I lie
    Parceled abroad in sound and hue,
    Dispersed through all I love.

I must go far away to a still place
And draw the shadows down across my eyes
   And wait and listen there

For wings vibrating from beyond the stars,
Wide-ranging, swiftly winnowing wings
Bearing me back mine own.

So soon, now, I shall lie deep hidden away
From sound or sight, with hearing strangely dull
And heavy-lidded eyes,—
'Tis time, O passionate soul, for me to go
Some far, hill-folded road apart
And learn the ways of peace.

Odell Shepard.

SHIP OF THE YEARS

Too slowly the Ship of the Years from dreamy
    horizons is drifting.
Blow on her sagging sails, oh winds, speeding her
    wings toward the west;—
The west where the Evening star her candle is
    quietly lifting,
Where a lonely bird is flying and crying that peace
    is best.

I, like a lonely bird, am weary of my heart's wild
    beating;
Weary of youth with its splendor and laughter and
    love that are pain.
I would seal my ears to the call that the mating
    larks are repeating;
I would blind my eyes to the rose, to the light of
    the April rain.

Oh youth, sweet youth, you are cruel, too cruel-
    sweet for bearing:
I would sit in the moonlight all unhurt by dreams,
    with peaceful breath.
Sail swifter, Ship of the Years, swifter! I would be
    faring
To the haven where with a quiet heart I may look
    in the face of Death.

Mary Sinton Leitch.

THE GRAY NORNS

What do you bring in your sacks, Gray Girls?
  "Sea-sand and sorrow."
What is the mist that behind you whirls?
  "The souls of to-morrow."

What are those shapes on the windy coasts?
  "The dead souls going."
But what are the loads on the backs of the ghosts?
  "The seed of their sowing."

Edwin Markham.

HAVE YOU FORGOTTEN HOW THAT
JUGGLER——FATE

Have you forgotten how that juggler—Fate,
Tossing the brittle balls of happiness,
Broke all of them and mocked at our distress,
When, back to earth you came, alas, too late!
I was a gray-haired Counselor of State,
You were a princess, and each shining tress
Was burnished gold to crown your loveliness—
Gray locks and golden do not match or mate.
With outstretched hands you, smiling, came to me,
Crossing the cruel chasm of the years.
I was too wise to hope, and spite of tears
We said farewell under a leafless tree
In a dead garden, 'neath a dying moon,
When you were born too late, and I too soon.

William Lindsey.

THE GHOST

One whom I loved and never can forget
  Returned to me in dream, and spoke with me,
  As audibly, as sweet familiarly
As though warm fingers twined warm fingers yet.
Her eyes were bright and with great wonder wet
  As in old days when some strange, swift decree
  Brought touch-close love or death; and sorrow-
      free
She spoke, as one long purged of all regret.

I heard, oh, glad beyond all speech, I heard;
  Till to my lips the flaming query flashed:
    How is it—over there? Then, quite undone,
She trembled; in her deep eyes like a bird
  The gladness fluttered, and as one abashed
    She shook her head bewildered, and was gone.

Hermann Hagedorn.

THE MOTH

Moth, on thy gilded wings,
Close where the lily springs,
  I saw thee flying.
Here by my candle light,
Wingless you lie to-night,
  Wingless and dying.

How like to souls afar
Viewing a burning star,
  Yearning and sighing.
How like star-pinioned dreams,
Foiled on the lesser beams,
  Visionless lying.

Robert Earl Brownlee.

THE UNSEEN WORLD

We never dreamed it was so near,
   And yet we might have known
Had we surmised from what bright sphere
   The viewless wings had flown,
      Or seen above her cradled head
      A mist-like, shining halo spread.

But round her pillowed helplessness
   Some wistful influence
Wove its soft spell, nor could we guess
   What beckonings lured her hence,
      Till through the fond, enfolding skies
      She vanished back to Paradise.

James B. Kenyon.

DIRGE

(From "Lilith")

O lay her gently where the lark is nesting
  And wingéd things are glad.
Tears end, and now begins the time of resting
  For her whose heart was sad.

Give roses, but a fairer bloom is taken.
  Strew lilies—she was one,
Gone in her silence to a place forsaken
  By roses and the sun.

Deep is her slumber at the last of sorrow,
  Of twilight and the rain.
Her eyes have closed forever on to-morrow
  And on to-morrow's pain.

George Sterling.

ON A DEAD MOTH

Who knows what trouble trembled in that throat,
　What sweet distraction for the summer moon,
That lured you out, a frail, careering boat,
　Across the midnight's purple, deep lagoon!
Some fire of madness lit that tiny brain,
　Some soft propulsion clouded through your breast,
And lifted you, a white and moving stain,
　Against the dark of that disastrous quest.

The sadness of all brief and lovely things,
　The fine and futile passions that we bear,
Haunt the bright wreck of your too fragile wings,
　And win a pity for you, ended there,—
Like us, hurled backward to the final shade,
From mad adventures for a moon or maid.

David Morton.

202

ONE BY ONE, ONE BY ONE

One by one, one by one,
Stitches of the hours run
Through the fine seams of the day,
Till like a garment it is done
And laid away.

One by one the days go by,
And suns climb up and down the sky;
One by one their seams are run—
As Time's untiring fingers ply
And life is done.

Hazel Hall.

Death comes like this, I know—
Snow-soft and gently cold;
Impalpable battalions of thin mist,
Light-quenching and sound-smothering and slow.

Slack as a wind-spilled sail
The spent world flaps in space—
Day's but a grayer night, and the old sun
Up the blind sky goes heavily and pale.

Out of all circumstance
I drift or seem to drift
In a vague vapor-world that clings and veils
Great trees arow like kneeling elephants.

How vast your voice is grown
That was so silver-soft;
Dim dies the candle-glory of your face—
Though we go hand in hand, I am alone.

Now Love and all the warm
Pageant of livingness
Trouble my quiet like forgotten dreams
Of ancient thunder on the hills of storm.

How loud, how terribly
Aflame are lights and sounds!
And yet beyond the fog I know there are
But lonely bells across gray wastes of sea.

John Reed.

L'ENVOI

Where are the loves that we have loved before
When once we are alone, and shut the door?
No matter whose the arms that held me fast,
The arms of Darkness hold me at the last.
No matter what the primrose path I tend,
I kiss the lips of Silence in the end.
No matter on what heart I found delight,
I come again unto the breast of Night.
No matter when or how love did befall,
'Tis Loneliness that loves me best of all,
And in the end she claims me, and I know
That she will stay, though all the rest may go.
No matter whose the eyes that I would keep
Near in the dark, 'tis in the eyes of Sleep
That I must look and look forevermore,
When once I am alone, and shut the door.

Willa Cather.

INDEX OF AUTHORS